America's
Farm Crisis

AMERICA'S FARM CRISIS

by Carol Gorman

Franklin Watts   New York/London/Toronto/Sydney   An Impact Book   1987

338.1
GOR

Graphs from "Outlook '87 Charts," U.S. Department of
Agriculture, Economic Research Service, December 1986.

Photographs courtesy of: USDA: pp. 16, 23 (bottom), 29, 37, 46
(June Davidek), 50 (Doug Wilson), 114 (A. L. Weeks); AP/Wide World
Photos: pp. 20, 31, 34, 58, 63, 65, 88; Iowa Department of Economic
Development: pp. 23 (top), 42, 92; Nick Elgar/LGI: p. 71; Charles Harbutt,
Archive Pictures, Inc.: p. 79; Magnum Photos, Inc.: pp. 96, 104 (Eugene
Richards), 99 (Gilles Peress); National 4-H Council: p. 98; Ron Evenson,
UNR College of Agriculture: p. 110.

Library of Congress Cataloging-in-Publication Data

Gorman, Carol.
America's farm crisis.

(An Impact book)
Bibliography: p.
Includes index.
Summary: Surveys the history of American farming since the 1960s
and examines the effects of the farm crisis on different segments of
the population.
1. Family farms—United States.   2. Farmers—United States.
3. Agriculture—Economic aspects—United States.   [1. Farms.
2. Farmers.   3. Agriculture—Economic aspects]   I. Title.
HD1476.U5G67 1987   338.1'0973   87-2087
ISBN 0-531-10408-7

Acknowledgments

I would like to acknowledge Gilbert C. Fite and his book, *American Farmers: The New Minority*, which proved to be an invaluable source of information about agricultural history.

Many people contributed information for this book, and I would like to thank them here. Les Santee, Karla Wright Maxwell, and Charmion Zieman provided information and read parts of the manuscript. Howard Mueller, "Master Farmer" from Waverly, Iowa; Diane Nitschke, the Winnieshiek County representative for JTPA; Karen Brown, the Howard County representative for JTPA; Joanne Dvorak, the coordinator at Family Service Agency in Cedar Rapids; and Fran Phillips, the Rural Hotline Coordinator, all gave generously of their time and expertise to provide additional information. Linda Bigley, Home Economist at the Linn County, Iowa Extension Service; Donna Wagner, office assistant at the East Central Iowa Area Extension Service at Cedar Rapids; and Barb Abbot, Communications Specialist at the Iowa State Extension Service provided invaluable assistance in locating agricultural experts and statistics.

Contents

For Ray Puechner,
and he knows why

*America's
Farm Crisis*

America's Farm Crisis

1

Thirteen-year-old Jennifer lives with her mother, father, and older brother on a 320-acre farm in southeastern Iowa. Farming is the only life she has ever known. In fact, it's the only life her father has ever known, and his father before him. Jennifer's great-grandfather homesteaded a piece of their farmland in the early part of this century, breaking the soil with a plow pulled by a team of horses. The farm was gradually turned over to the sons in the family who joined their father working in the fields.

Jennifer helps in the day-to-day farm operations along with her brother, Joe. She helps her dad and Joe feed the hogs every morning and evening, spreading the lines of corn from the feed sacks along the cement floor outside the hog sheds. In the spring while Joe and his dad "work up the land" with the harrow and plant the corn, Jennifer and her mother plant the large family garden in the backyard. They grow many of the vegetables their family will eat throughout the year. In the fall, Jennifer and her mother will can beans, beets, and tomatoes.

Jennifer rides the school bus to a consolidated junior-senior high school. Students from several small towns in the area are bussed in every day during the school year. Most of the teachers and the principal live in a larger city 40 miles (64 km) away and commute in car pools. During planting or harvesting time, there are fewer kids in school, because they are needed to help in the fields. At the high school level, students can take agriculture education classes along with the regular curriculum. In these courses, students learn up-to-date farming methods that will help them in the future when they take over the operation of their family farms.

Jennifer loves farm life and can't imagine living any other way. She loves living close to nature, watching the changing seasons, and helping her father, mother, and brother run the farm.

Life had been good for Jennifer's family for as long as she could remember. They had everything they needed, like food and clothing, and they always were able to keep their farm machinery in good repair. The bank was willing to loan the family money every year in the spring for seed and fertilizer, and Jennifer's father was always able to repay the loan in the fall after his crops had been harvested and sold. Farming had always been their life, and to do anything else was unimaginable.

At least that was the way things were up until a few years ago. Jennifer isn't sure how it all happened, but life began to change drastically for her family and for many of their friends and neighbors.

Jennifer's parents whisper a lot now about having serious financial problems. Jennifer hears them and worries. She wishes they would talk to her and Joe about what is happening. Because of their troubles, her parents are on edge, and they've begun to quarrel with each other, which worries Jennifer even more than the whispering. Lately, they've begun to yell at her and Joe, even when there is no reason for it.

Jennifer's father says he should never have expanded his farming operation back when Jennifer was little. He blames himself for their lack of money. Jennifer wonders if her mother blames him, too.

Her mother has recently found a full-time job in town to help earn some money for the family. Jennifer knows this hurts her father; he has always been a proud man who thinks a husband should be able to support his family.

Jennifer's mother begins each morning at 5:00 A.M., early enough to do her housework and get the farm bookkeeping up-to-date before her thirty minute drive into town to her job. When she returns at night, she and Jennifer fix supper. After the kitchen is cleaned up, Jennifer's mother drags herself to bed so she can get up the next morning and start all over again. Jennifer hardly sees her anymore.

Jennifer hears talk about the neighbors' troubles, too. A family down the road has started buying groceries with food stamps. She knows many farmers who have had to sell part of their livestock or machinery to help pay off debts, and several have lost their entire farms.

The most disturbing news came from the next county where a farmer was so depressed over his financial problems that he killed himself. Jennifer watches her father anxiously and wonders if he might do the same thing. She has a hard time concentrating on classwork, and her grades have suffered.

Many of Jennifer's classmates are having the same problems. At first some of the kids confided only in their closest friends. But after the teachers became aware of how many students were experiencing serious problems at home, they began encouraging class discussions about farm and home problems. Jennifer thought it helped to hear that others were going through the same things, to get it out in the open. If only her parents

*America's farms are
facing a difficult time.*

would share their feelings with her and Joe, it would help even more.

Jennifer wonders what will happen to her family and the farm, and she wonders if farm life will ever be happy and secure again.

How did this happen to Jennifer's family? Why are other farmers having severe financial problems? The majority of American farmers are financially healthy, but a growing number of them share the problems that Jennifer's family is facing. Is there a solution to their dilemma? The farm situation raises difficult questions, and there are no easy answers.

In this book we'll examine these important questions along with several solutions suggested by farmers and farm critics. We'll consider why these solutions have not satisfied everyone. The farm problem is a complicated one, even for the experts, but we will examine the important issues necessary for a basic understanding of the American farm crisis.

The Farmer:
No Stranger to Hard Times

2

Farm products have long been an important part of American trade. Some farmers can remember when, in 1929, nearly $2 billion worth of agricultural products were sent to other countries. This was 35 percent of all exported American *commodities*, or goods, and 10 percent of the country's income.[1]

But surprisingly, in that same year the average farmer earned a net income of only $273, compared with the national average of $750.[2]

How could farmers, who were such a large part of America's economy, have earned so little for themselves? To answer that, let's look at an important rule of economics, *the law of supply and demand*. When the amount of goods (in this case, farm products) is greater than the public's demand for the goods, the sellers (farmers) have to lower their prices to stimulate sales.

Farmers had little to say about how much money they could get for their products. Prices were determined by what others were willing to pay. After a farmer had harvested his wheat, he took it to a grain elevator to be sold and stored there. When there was a good harvest of grain in the area, and all of the farmers had an abundance of wheat to sell, the buyer at the elevator could offer a lower price for wheat, knowing that the farmers would have to sell it at the offered price. This price might not be high enough to cover all of a farmer's expenses, much less give him a profit.

Farmers needed a fair exchange ratio between the farm products they were selling and the nonfarm items they needed to buy. This came to be called *parity*. Farmers couldn't achieve parity in the 1930s when they received low prices for their goods and had to pay relatively high prices for nonfarm items.

The farmer couldn't bargain alone; there was always another farmer willing to sell his grain for the price offered at the elevator. Most farmers were fiercely independent and not interested in organizing to control the amount of product they produced. Theoretically, according to the law of supply and demand, if they had organized themselves, they could have voluntarily decreased the supply, so they would receive more money for their crops.

During the Depression in the 1930s, when many Americans were poor, the financial situation for farmers became worse. In 1932, the average *net income* (after all expenses had been paid) of people living on farms was just $74 a year.[3] And the farmer received only 58 percent parity. In other words, for every dollar he spent on nonfarm items, he received just fifty-eight cents for his farm goods.[4]

An organization formed in 1920 played an important role in the development of legislation to help the farmer. The American Farm Bureau, an organization of farm families, pushed for legislation to help the troubled farmer. Their efforts were rewarded in 1933 when Franklin D. Roosevelt's administration passed the Agricultural Adjustment Act, which was designed according to the law of supply and demand. It encouraged farmers to produce less food by reducing the number of acres of

During the Depression, a group of Iowa farmers protested at the state capitol to demand relief from taxes and debts through legislation.

certain crops, thereby driving up the prices for these products. Since most of the farmers had already planted their fields when the law was passed, they were paid to plow under some of their crops and to promise to reduce their production during the next two years. The government agreed to pay parity prices for crops from farmers participating in this reduction program. Soon after, hog farmers were asked to slaughter their baby pigs and pregnant sows. In addition, the law stated that the government would store surplus crops so that this produce might be available later in poor harvest years, and the farmers received the value of these stored crops as a loan. If market prices didn't reach the price of the loan, the farmer could just turn over his crop to the newly organized Commodity Credit Corporation as repayment on the loan. This law is an example of a *price support*.

Other laws were passed to help the struggling farmer. Those who couldn't pay the mortgage on their farms were given help with Title II of the Agricultural Adjustment Act. This law helped them to *refinance*, or to make different arrangements for the payments on their farms. In 1934, the Frazier-Lemke Farm Bankruptcy Act was passed by Congress giving many farmers near ruin a five-year period during which lenders, such as banks, could not *foreclose*, or sell at auction, their farms. This is called a *moratorium* on foreclosures. (In 1935, the act was declared unconstitutional. The Farm Mortgage Moratorium Act of 1935 then provided for a three-year moratorium.)

Many thousands of farmers were saved from losing their farms because of these laws. Between 1933 and 1940, over $4.5 billion was paid directly to American farmers.[5]

Not all Americans agreed that farmers should be helped by the government. Many people felt that farmers should not be paid because they were having financial difficulties. After all, they pointed out, the government doesn't step in and rescue a businessman who is nearly bankrupt. This controversy continues today with strong arguments on both sides of the issue. We'll explore these arguments later in this book.

Even though farmers had reduced the amount of land they planted, there was still too much food being produced to raise the amount of money farmers received for their crops. Net farm income was up to $685 by 1940,[6] but this was still much too low to give many farmers a decent living.

Farming methods changed a great deal during the 1920s, 1930s, and 1940s because of the increased use of fertilizers, insecticides, and herbicides, and because of innovations in farm machinery. The switch from horse-drawn machinery to tractors allowed many more crops to be planted in a shorter amount of time. Tractors were faster and covered more ground. The land that used to be reserved for grazing the horses and mules that pulled the farm machinery could be plowed up and planted. After the crops were harvested, the food could be transported quickly to market in cars and trucks. The low prices that farmers received for their goods encouraged farmers to cut their costs by using these labor-saving machines. But only the more successful farmers could afford such luxuries.

Since the smaller farmer couldn't afford these new machines, he couldn't compete. The result was that many small farms were sold off and absorbed into the larger, more prosperous operations.

Even though fewer acres were being planted by farmers because of the federal programs that encour-

The change from horse-drawn machinery to tractors allowed more crops to be planted.

aged reduction of productive land, such innovations as increased mechanization, the use of chemicals, and more efficient farming methods kept farm output at a steady, if not increasing, level.

During World War II in the 1940s, farmers were encouraged by the government to increase their output. The war gave farmers a level of prosperity they had never before experienced. At the beginning of the war, farm prices were at 77 percent parity but soon rose to full parity and higher.[7] Some farmers were able to buy up the land they had lost during hard times in the Depression.

But after the war was over, and the United States returned to a peace economy, the old problems came back. There were too many farm products available and not enough demand to absorb them to keep the prices at a profit level for farmers.

The Korean War took care of some of the farm surplus products, but it was again a temporary solution to the old farm problem.

The farm debates continued through the Eisenhower administration during the 1950s, particularly over whether price supports (and what kind of supports) should be available to farmers. Government officials argued that it was the largest farms (needing money the least) that benefitted the most, with little of the money going to the smaller farmers. Congress finally passed a law in 1956 that paid farmers of certain basic crops (corn, wheat, peanuts, rice, cotton, and tobacco) to *reserve*, or keep out of production, part of their farmland. However, this measure didn't solve the problem of overproduction. The cost of this type of program was staggering. In 1958–59 the total cost of farm programs reached $4.6 billion. Hundreds of millions of dollars were spent just to store surplus grain.[8]

During the administrations of presidents John F. Kennedy and Lyndon B. Johnson in the 1960s, farmers

24 —

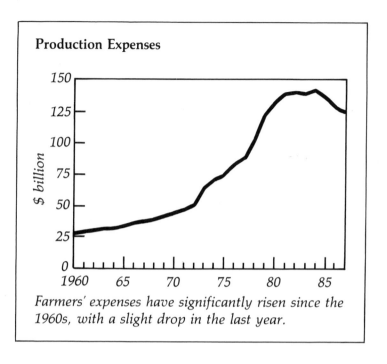

Production Expenses

Farmers' expenses have significantly risen since the 1960s, with a slight drop in the last year.

were again given money to take part of their land out of production. In addition, steps were taken to expand the farm export market, particularly to Japan and Western Europe. During these years, a farmer's per capita income rose from approximately 50 percent to 75 percent of that of a nonfarm worker.[9]

As modern agriculture continued to improve methods of farming and successful farms continued to grow in size, more and more of the small, family-run farms sold out to the larger, more efficient operations. Between 1954 and 1960, the number of farms decreased by 911,000.[10]

During the latter part of the 1960s, farm policy continued as it had before, with price supports not meeting what the farmer had to pay in expenses.

Because of their continued economic hardship, many farmers concluded that the only way to increase their income was to expand their operations by buying more land, and to cut their costs per unit by using better, more efficient equipment. In other words, they would grow more food, and spend more money producing it, but at a less expensive rate per food item.

This heavy expansion by farmers is a major contributing factor to the crisis American farmers are facing today. In the next chapter, we'll look at some of the choices made by farmers in the 1960s and 1970s and see how those choices, along with advice from government officials and local banks, led them into the rural crisis of the 1980s.

The Sixties
and Seventies

3

In the 1960s and 1970s, farms continued to decline in number and increase in size and efficiency. Farmers, in effect, had to become business managers to successfully handle their expanding operations. Without good management, a farm was certain to fail.

Some farmers successfully reduced labor costs by investing in larger machinery to do the jobs workers used to do. New tractors could cover larger areas in a shorter amount of time, so the farmer could take advantage of a brief period of good weather to plant or harvest his crops.

Other new management techniques included increasing the use of improved chemical fertilizers, insecticides and herbicides, and new strains of crops. The modern farmer also could have invested in a computer system to help him keep track of his increasingly more complicated financial records.

Much of the research in agriculture was taking place at land-grant universities around the country. In the Morrill Act of 1862, Congress had granted every state 30,000 acres of land for every senator and representative in Washington. The law required that the land be sold. Proceeds from the sales were to establish and maintain agricultural colleges and universities. The research, teaching, and extension functions of these land-grant schools have proved invaluable and the key to agricultural technology and advancement.

Land values increased during the 1960s, climbing an average of 4 to 6 percent every year.[1] This encouraged farmers who could afford it to buy more land, using the land they already owned as collateral. In fact, because farmers received low prices for their crops, expansion was necessary just to maintain the same income level year after year. Many farmers were worth a great deal of money, but it was because their land was so valuable. The only way they could spend that money was to sell some of their land.

Farmers realized they could earn more money for themselves and their families by buying and planting more land and spreading their costs over a larger area to raise more food. In 1959 the size of an average farm was 404 acres; by 1974 it had increased to 534 acres.[2]

While the large farms continued to grow, the situation for the smaller farms became worse. Since price supports and land reduction payments were figured in terms of numbers of acres and farm output, most of the support money went to the most successful farms, while the small farms received little or nothing, just as before.

This was another of the major criticisms of federal support to farmers, that the money went where it was needed the least. Critics pointed out that between 1964 and 1974, half of all government payments to farmers

In the 1960s and 1970s, farm equipment became bigger and more costly.

went to the 20 percent of farmers earning the highest income.

These same critics argued that the United States shouldn't be helping the farmers who were increasing their yields anyway, since overproduction was a major contributor to the country's farm problems.

In the 1960s and 1970s the farmer's expenses skyrocketed. Farm equipment became bigger, more efficient, more comfortable to use, and much more expensive. A farmer could count on spending as much as $20,000 for a large tractor in 1970. By 1980, the largest models sold for $60,000 to $100,000. A farmer could owe the bank several hundred thousand dollars just for farm machinery alone.[3]

The early 1970s saw continued federal help for the farmer. The Agriculture Act of 1970 continued to assure minimum prices for basic farm products, and in 1971 Congress appropriated $8.1 billion for the Department of Agriculture.

Farmers had some good news in the 1960s and 1970s, as the United States crop exports increased. In the mid-1960s, when this country harvested 300 million acres of farmland, 50–70 million acres worth of crops were marketed to other countries. This number continued to rise.[4]

In the summer of 1972, the Soviet Union had a very poor harvest. Their misfortune led to some of the best agricultural years American farmers had seen. The Soviets needed the farm crops to feed their people and livestock, and they bought $750 million worth of wheat and feed grains from the United States.

A Russian grain ship waiting to be loaded during the massive U.S.-Soviet Union grain deal in 1972

Their purchase caused other countries to look toward the United States for grain. Suddenly, the amount of American exports skyrocketed. In a short time, our stores of hundreds of thousands of grain bins filled with surplus crops were nearly all sold. Farmers who had stored crops on their own land were able to sell them for prices unheard of just a year before.

In addition, media attention was focused heavily on world hunger after leading agricultural experts began reporting in 1974 the first signs of a food shortage crisis that could reach "disastrous proportions before the year is out." These experts didn't agree on how long this emergency would last. Some thought food shortages were caused by a lack of fertilizer, and that the situation would stabilize in four to six years. Others predicted decades of "unrelenting misery."[5]

The *New York Times* reported in September 1974 that, because of a poor wheat crop in India, "millions may starve in the next few months." Many authorities thought that to give relief to India would cut too deeply into America's already low grain reserves, and that Americans would be forced to change their diets to free food resources for that country and other parts of the world.

President Gerald Ford addressed the United Nations, calling for a "global strategy" to deal with the food shortage. The *New York Times*, the day after Ford's speech, stated, "Recognizing that the United States is the world's largest supplier of food, or as some put it, 'We are the Arabs of the food business,' Mr. Ford drew parallels between this country's responsibility on world food supplies and the Arab position on world energy supplies."

In the face of this tremendous demand, government officials now urged American farmers to grow more to feed the hungry world. During this time wheat prices increased by 300 percent.

Nineteen seventy-three and 1974 were agriculture's boom years. Many farmers paid off their earlier debts and took out new loans to buy more land, build new and bigger houses for their families, and improve their farm buildings. They bought bigger, more efficient machinery to work the new acres of land.

The good years for the farmers in the mid-1970s led to an increase in food prices. American consumers were angered at the higher prices they saw in the supermarkets, and they demanded that the government place an *embargo* on grain sales to the Soviet Union. That meant they wanted to stop grain exports to that country. Consumers hoped that restricting farm exports would bring food prices down. President Ford's administration did bow to public pressure and limited sales until the effect on American consumers could be determined. Then the farmers were upset, so the Ford administration drew up a five-year agreement with the Soviet Union that had provisions protecting American consumers against rising food prices.

Even though he had repeatedly promised not to interfere with food exports, when President Jimmy Carter took office, he did place limitations on beef sold to other countries when high beef prices angered American consumers.

Carter again broke his promise to farmers, in 1979, when, to protest the Soviet Union's invasion of Afghanistan, he refused to complete a planned sale of 17 million tons of grain to that country. American farmers felt betrayed, even though many of them patriotically endorsed the president's action against the communist country. The farmers didn't like being used in international politics when the result affected their livelihood.

Thurman Gaskill, president of the Iowa Corn Promotion Board, said in an interview with the *Des Moines Register*, "The Carter administration is using the [em-

In the late 1970s, farmers protested in Washington against low farm prices.

bargo] at the expense of Iowa farmers." Gaskill didn't think the action would be effective anyway, because the Soviets could buy the needed grain from other countries.[6]

Even though Carter assured the farmers that they wouldn't be affected by the embargo, that the government would buy up the grain that would have been sold to the Soviets, grain prices did fall. Many farmers had to sell their goods at depressed prices just to get enough money together to plant the next spring's crop.

During 1975 and 1976, farmers received lower prices for their crops, but their situation was still quite good. Expenses were still tremendously high, though, particularly for the farmers who were paying off new equipment or new houses. They could continue to make the payments on their loans, but only if high crop prices remained.

When prices did fall, the effects were disastrous for many farmers. The price of wheat fell from $6.00 to $1.80 per bushel. Farmers may have had to spend as much as $3.50 per bushel to raise the wheat.[7] At the same time expenses continued to rise. In 1977 production costs climbed 7 to 10 percent.[8] Farmers were not only paying their operating expenses, but also living expenses for their families, taxes, and the interest and principal on their loans.

Farmers became desperate. Many of them joined together to form the American Agricultural Movement. They planned a farmers' strike if Congress did not pass legislation by December 14, 1977, to provide them with prices at 100 percent parity. Their plan was to stand together and stop planting crops and buying nonfarm goods, hoping that the public outcry would force Congress to act on their behalf.

The American Agricultural Movement became famous for organizing marches and rallies to draw attention to the farm problem. People formed what became known as "tractorcades," long lines of tractors in the streets and on the highways that rolled into large cities, drawing media attention and giving farmers a chance to publicly criticize farm policies and demand 100 percent parity. Many tractorcades traveled to Washington, D.C. and demonstrated in front of the nation's capital.

The farmers certainly attracted attention with their tractorcades, but not all of it was sympathetic to their plight. In a *New York Times* article in 1980, Representative Peter A. Peyser criticized the demonstrations. "By my calculations," he said, "the farmers will have spent some $215,000 on fuel alone to make their point in Washington. Add to this the millions of dollars these farmers will spend during their stay, and I say that this type of demonstration does not speak well for a supposedly impoverished industry."[9]

The American Agricultural Movement's planned strike fizzled out without much commotion. The parity legislation was not passed. Some farmers participated in the refusal to buy and sell nonfarm goods, but for the most part, it was business as usual.

Farmers had gained some ground in their campaign. The Food and Agriculture Act of 1977 raised the price supports on some crops, and $900 million was provided to farmers who had little money to buy necessary items. The Farmers Home Administration, a government agency which makes loans to farmers, took over some of the unstable loans made by small country banks and provided additional loans to farmers.[10]

These measures did not satisfy the farmers, however. They still demanded 100 percent parity and continued to exert pressure on Congressional members.

A grain silo

Finally, in May of 1978, a bill was passed by Congress. It did not provide 100 percent parity, but it did achieve several things, among them a $4 billion emergency loan program and what amounted to a moratorium on foreclosures by the Farmers Home Administration.[11]

By early 1979 conditions had improved for farmers. But they were losing public support because of inflation and rising food prices. When farmers again urged Congress for more favorable prices—90 percent parity this time—consumers cried no. They argued that such a measure would increase food prices, and they were already paying too much for food. Congress agreed.

Then a different kind of problem surfaced in the late 1970s. Foreign investors began buying large areas of American farmland. In 1978, $80 million worth of land was purchased by wealthy foreign buyers. Many of them were Western Europeans who would have had to pay twice the price for prime farmland in their own countries. Their governments provided tax breaks for buying land in this country.

It was relatively easy for foreigners to make these purchases in the United States, because the deals did not have to be reported to the government. A government agency that tried to find out exactly how much farmland belonged to foreigners had a difficult time tracking down ownership records. Under pressure from farmers and the American Agricultural Movement, Congress passed the Agricultural Foreign Investment Disclosure Act in 1978. It required foreigners to report the purchase of any farmland to the Agricultural Stabilization and Conservation Service in its local county office.

Farmers were concerned about foreign investors for several reasons. One of the most fundamental was that they didn't want to see the American farms, which throughout our nation's history have belonged primarily to American families, come under the control of people outside of this country. Another reason was their concern for the future of farming, particularly at a time when small American farmers were going under and their land was being taken over by large corporate farms.

As the 1970s drew to a close, farmers were suffering from rising inflation and relatively low prices for their crops. Some farmers thought that the increasing value of their land was the only thing keeping them from financial ruin. They didn't know then that the near future would bring even harder times. In the next chapter, we'll explore what has happened in the 1980s.

The Eighties:
The Crisis

4

By the 1980s the number of acres of American farmland used for food production had dropped severely to 1,047 million acres, down from 1,161 million acres in 1955. That meant that in the years between 1955 and 1980, an average of 6 million acres had been taken out of production every year.[1]

It might be thought that this decline in the use of farmland would certainly help the farmers receive better prices for their crops. But even though less acreage was planted, production continued to rise because of the increasing use of modern farm technology.

It was becoming more difficult for farmers to get loans. When farmers needed to borrow money in the spring for seed or fertilizer, or for repairs on their machinery, they went to a bank or other lending institution to get a loan. They had to pay interest on that loaned money. In the late 1970s, farmers could get a loan and pay around 8 percent interest on their money. But every year the interest rates rose, and by 1980 farmers were paying as much as 17 to 20 percent on the money they borrowed.[2]

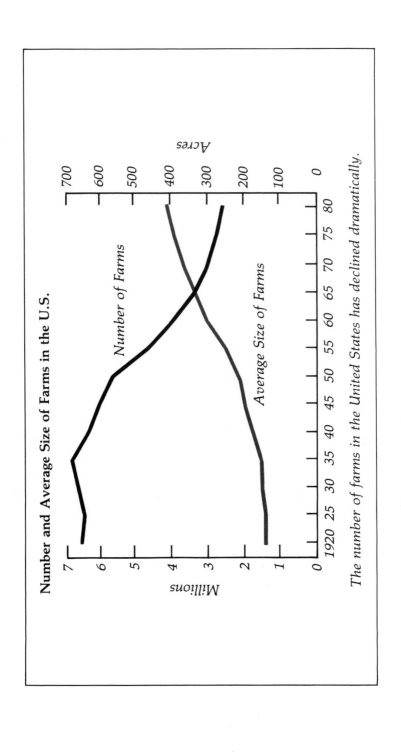

Number and Average Size of Farms in the U.S.

Acres

700
600
500
400
300
200
100
0

Number of Farms

Average Size of Farms

1920 25 30 35 40 45 50 55 60 65 70 75 80

0 1 2 3 4 5 6 7

Millions

The number of farms in the United States has declined dramatically.

Purchasing more sophisticated equipment and machinery caused many farmers to go into debt.

Some institutions began refusing to lend money to farmers who wanted to buy new equipment. A farmer's desire for new machinery was thought by these lenders to be extravagant when there were so many other farmers who needed money for such necessities as feeding livestock and taking care of crops. Other lenders extended credit only to their best customers. And *any* farmer had to prove that he would be able to pay back the loan by a specific date before he could receive the loaned money.

Many farmers needed money to plant crops because they hadn't sold last year's grain. Port and rail strikes had prevented large numbers of farmers from selling their grain, which would have provided money for the 1980 crop. Farmers were urged to get part of the needed money by selling some of their stored grain now, instead of waiting for the prices to get better. Some farmers took a second mortgage on their farms or refinanced their current mortgages to cover their present production costs.

In addition to having difficulty obtaining loans, farmers also found themselves paying much more money for other necessities. Fuel for running tractors, cars, trucks, and combines—all necessary for farm operation—became very expensive. Crude oil prices had doubled in 1979, and by planting time in the spring of 1980, farmers were paying $1.10 per gallon for their diesel fuel, which was more than twice what they had paid a year earlier.[3] In 1980, the cost of fertilizer, seed, and farm chemicals shot up 20 percent.[4] Farmers tried to cut some of these costs by using less fertilizer or by cultivating less, running the tractor over the soil twice instead of four or five times.

One banker commented that for many farmers a good year would be to just break even and keep their farms together.

Even though many farmers harvested the same crops and bought the same farm items they had bought a year earlier, some of them were worth as much as $20,000 less because of the increased costs in running their farms. To add to their misery, the worth of their land began to decline. This made it even more difficult for farmers to get loans, because many of them used their land as collateral.

Even when the U.S. Federal Reserve Board handed over $3 billion to the banking system to help farmers and small businessmen suffering from the crisis, there was little noticeable effect. Many farmers and lenders began comparing their financial situation to the Great Depression of the 1930s. Farm debt jumped to a high of $158 billion, up by $76 billion in five years.[5]

Hog and poultry production rose sharply in the early 1980s, glutting the market and sending prices down. Consumers in America and Europe were all hit hard by the slowing economy and responded by buying more pork and poultry, and less beef. Also, people were eating less beef because of its high cholesterol level. The cattle feeders felt the pinch as did the grain farmers since less grain was needed to feed the cattle.

As costs jumped higher and higher for the farmer, he was receiving less for his farm goods. Average prices for all farm items by the middle of 1980 were running 6 percent lower than the previous year. Wheat cost an average $4.60 per bushel to grow, and the farmer received only about $3.50 per bushel to grow it. Corn cost about $2.65 per bushel to grow, and that was about 25 cents per bushel more than the farmer was paid for it.[6]

In a July 1980 article in *Business Week*, Gene Futrell, an economist at Iowa State University, said that even though many farmers had had rough times in the last several years, the troubles that farmers were seeing in 1980 were different. He said that in past years, the farmers experiencing financial problems were those who had borrowed heavily for new equipment, new houses, and more land. But now, he said, everyone was experiencing the cost-price squeeze because interest rates and all other costs had climbed so high.

Farmers were not the only people experiencing high costs. Inflation was affecting consumers all over the country. Americans didn't like the rise in food prices, but two-thirds of what they paid at the supermarket went to labor, transportation, packaging, and merchandising costs. The farmer was only receiving a third of the food dollar.

The summer of 1980 also saw a severe drought in some southern, eastern, and midwestern states. Some cotton farmers in the South collected only four-tenths of a bale per acre, compared to a full bale the year before. Corn was badly damaged, and many farmers planted additional acres of winter wheat to make up for their losses. The result was a record wheat crop, which sent prices skidding down by 12 percent.

Early in 1981, the Reagan administration, in an attempt to curtail government spending, revealed plans to chop $7.6 billion out of farm funds. Agriculture Secretary John R. Block also announced that recommendations would be made to Congress to end target price supports, the program that paid farmers when prices of grain fell below predetermined levels.[7] The projected savings from these cuts was to be only $285 million over the next three years, but government officials pointed out that the farm program was economically risky. They reminded their critics that in 1979, when prices fell, it cost the government $1 billion in payments to farmers.[8]

Besides, the government officials said, the big, successful farmers are doing so well that assistance should not be needed anymore. The Agriculture Department reported that 40 percent of all crops in the United States

*A drought like this can destroy
a farmer's entire crop.*

were grown by 2.4 percent of the nation's farms, and they earned an average of $200,000 or more a year. So why did they need help?[9]

The Reagan administration had a long and bitter battle on its hands. One of the projects the administration objected to the most was the milk-price-support program that required the federal government to buy excess dairy products to keep prices low. For three years the government had bought 796 million pounds of dried milk, 220 million pounds of butter, and 559 million pounds of cheese. This food had been stored, and the bill to the taxpayers was a staggering $1.8 billion.[10] After much debate and maneuvering, a compromise was proposed in the House of Representatives. Backed by the powerful dairy lobby, it reduced but still maintained price supports for milk.

Exports did well in 1981, reaching a record $46 billion.[11] In April, President Reagan lifted the partial embargo on sales to the Soviet Union that had been ordered by President Carter. But, in December, when the Soviets declared martial law in Poland, Reagan cut off talks with Moscow that were to call for a new, multi-year grain deal.

When the U.S. dollar is strong (when it takes more foreign money to equal the dollar's value), our country's exports decline. The reason for this is that, with a strong U.S. dollar, foreign countries have to pay more for our goods than for the goods of competing countries. So, instead of buying from the United States, they buy products from those countries that can sell the same products more cheaply. By the end of 1981, the dollar was becoming stronger, and the United States saw all of its exports, including farm products, declining.

At the end of 1981, interest rates began to come down slightly, but farm prices and orders for agricultural products didn't budge. This puzzled even the experts who had looked forward to falling interest rates, expecting the financial picture for farmers to improve.

By mid-1982, Democrats who were eyeing the upcoming Congressional elections scrambled to introduce "emergency" legislation favorable to farmers. One senator introduced a bill that would provide more loans to farmers and ranchers, raise wheat prices, and increase food supplies to Poland. Another senator led a push for new laws that would delay foreclosures and pay farmers to take land out of production.

Republicans urged President Reagan's administration to open talks with the Russians on future grain buys. In August 1982, Reagan announced that he was extending for one year a grain supply agreement with the Soviets that would permit them to purchase a minimum of 6 million tons of corn and wheat. However, meetings between the United States and Moscow would be necessary if they wanted to buy more than 8 million tons.

Farmers were disappointed. The Russians had just suffered through four bad harvest years in a row, and farmers were hoping that Washington would offer them a long-term deal guaranteeing sales for several years. The Soviet crop level was 68 million tons below their goal, which meant that they would be buying $6 billion worth of grain from somewhere.[12]

"We have simply invited the Soviet Union to shop elsewhere to fill in its shortages," said Robert Delano, president of the American Farm Bureau Federation, in a *Time* magazine interview.

Farm income continued its plunge downward. Grain growers were hurting the most, with corn producers at the top of the list. Wheat and soybean farmers came in close behind.

The Farmers Home Administration, usually a last resort lending institution for farmers, reported that the number of people behind in or not making payments on their loans jumped from 27.2 percent in 1981 to 33.6 percent in 1982.[13]

Many more farmers were forced to sell off part of their equipment, land, or livestock to make their payments. As their financial problems became worse, they continued to raise crops at record levels, which depressed prices even more. The cycle continued, and no one knew for sure how to end it.

Dairy producers, unlike grain farmers, were not limited to any maximum amount of milk they could produce. So they continued to produce up to 10 percent more than consumers were buying. And the government, required by law to purchase the surplus, paid $2.5 billion for it. A billion dollars worth of cheese and butter were given to needy people all over the country to help reduce the cost of storing these items. And dairy farmers continued to produce more, knowing the government would buy it.[14]

Wheat farmers, guaranteed a minimum price from the government of $4.05 per bushel, continued to raise more wheat, knowing that they would get that price and not the market price, which was $3.57 per bushel.[15] *U.S. News and World Report*, to dramatize the dimension of the surplus problem, stated that the amount of surplus wheat the government had to store could fill a train of 55,000 hopper cars stretching from Washington D.C. to Chicago, Illinois. Since loans were so hard to get with land values down (land values dropped 7.7 percent in 1981), farmers needed the cash flow, which was, in the short run, more important to holding the farm together than was the final price farmers received for their crops.

While Congress debated over legislation that would cut price-support programs, the farmers were arguing that a better solution would be to increase food exports and sell off the surplus farm goods. But because of worldwide recession and the strong American dollar,

*The third largest wheat crop
on record was in 1983.*

that option didn't look any more optimistic than it had the previous year.

Congress finally agreed to begin direct payments to farmers who would set aside and not plant some of their cropland.

There were two sides to this issue. The people who favored the set-aside program declared that it would raise market prices above the federal minimum levels. That, these supporters said, would cut the cost of the government's $9 billion grain subsidy. Critics of the program said that the land diversion payment barely covered a farmer's costs and didn't offer a farmer incentives to produce less.

To qualify for the program, farmers agreed to set aside 10 percent of their corn land and 15 percent of their wheat acreage. But few farmers signed up for the program. Many of them needed the cash and were willing to bet they could beat the subsidy price in the market. They were wrong, however, and they took a financial beating and produced a near-record wheat crop.

Grain storage facilities were bulging all over the country, leading some federal officials to consider utilizing unused railroad hopper cars to store some of the grain. The Department of Agriculture authorized $40 billion in loan money to farmers for on-farm storage, with a maximum of $25,000 per farm. Only the farmers who cooperated in the reduced-acreage program were eligible.

President Reagan also authorized selling the Soviet Union up to 23 million tons of grain. Many experts, however, doubted that the Soviets would buy that much.

Even though farmers were having trouble, many survived. In addition to government aid, farmers took necessary steps themselves. In some farm families the husband or wife—or both—found employment in town to help make ends meet. They repaired old equipment instead of buying new, and they used less fertilizer and fuel.

Some farmers were able to continue operating because they raised cattle or hogs, and prices for livestock had improved. Farmers with dairy cows continued to receive heavy subsidies.

The American Farm Bureau, made up of nearly 2 million families, continued to give considerable support to farmers. An independent organization of volunteers, it worked (and continues to work) at the local, state, and national levels. As the largest general farm organization in the country, it supported educational programs and lobbied for favorable legislation. And in many states, members were able to obtain insurance and get cooperative and group prices for farm supplies, and cooperative marketing of farm products.

The administration helped again when, in October 1982, it announced a new program to subsidize exports of farm goods and decrease interest rates on federally sponsored farm loans.

But farm income continued its decline in 1982, reaching only $19 billion, the lowest since the Depression. And that figure was not enough to even cover the cost of interest on all the money farmers owed, a staggering $200 billion.[16]

In December 1982, the federal government announced a new program designed to help farmers and reduce grain surpluses. This program, called the Payment in Kind—or PIK—program, called for farmers to set aside an additional 10 to 30 percent of their land on top of what they had idled for price supports. In return, they would receive some of the surplus crops that were being stored around the country. Farmers could then sell the crops for whatever they could get.

One might think that this would cause a grain glut on the market, causing prices to decline. But the reasoning behind this new program was this: farmers would actually receive *fewer* crops than they would be able to grow on the land that had been set aside. The total amount reaching the market, therefore, would be lowered, thereby reducing prices. There would be a benefit to the farmer, because he wouldn't have to spend money planting the crops on that much of his land.

Agriculture Secretary John Block hoped that by idling 20 percent of American farmland, the program could save up to $5 billion in price supports and storage fees during the next two to three years. Furthermore, he expected to bring grain supply and demand into balance in that length of time.

But many farm experts worried that support industries such as fertilizer companies and tractor manufacturers that employed as many as 50,000 workers would be hurt by a lack of business. Mass layoffs were feared.

Even though the farm suppliers went through hard times with the farmer, they were optimistic about the Payment in Kind program. They assumed that as the surpluses were reduced, the prices on farm goods would rise, and farmers would then have the money to buy supplies the following year.

Some farm implement dealers did offer special incentives to farmers, encouraging them to buy at 1982 sale prices, or putting off interest payments on some sales that were financed by the companies. But farmers were unable to purchase many of these machines, or farm chemicals, and the fears of the experts were soon realized.

By May 1983 it appeared as though agriculture would take an upturn. Fuel prices and interest rates were lower, the Soviet Union announced a desire to buy U.S. grain, and there was optimism about the new PIK program. Corn prices had jumped from $2 a bushel in January to $3 by late May, which helped even the farmers who did not participate in the program. The Agriculture Department was predicting that farm prices would be up by 3 percent that year.[17]

Many farmers were happy to have the extra cash so they could begin paying back their bank loans, which, for many farmers, was the biggest worry and biggest expense.

As it turned out, many more farmers than anticipated signed up for the PIK program. In fact, 77 million acres, which is *one-third of all eligible farmland* in the country, were idled.[18] As in earlier set-aside programs, farmers idled their least productive farmland and intensively planted their most fertile acres. As a result, wheat farmers produced the third-largest crop on record, 2.4 billion bushels.[19]

Farmers complained about the quality of grain they received in payment. Some of it was as much as two or three years old, taken from the government's surplus storage facilities. The cost of 1983 programs was approximately $22 billion, five times the amount spent on farm supports in 1981.[20] As had most earlier farm programs, the PIK program benefitted the largest, most prosperous farmers and corporations, some producers receiving as much as a million dollars' worth of surplus grain.

In addition, the amount of land the government would allow to be idled was based on a farmer's total acreage of planted and harvested land in previous years. In California the Department of Agriculture allowed cotton farmers who were benefiting from the PIK program to plant in between rows on land supposedly taken out of production.[21] Even though no law was broken, this practice was not in the spirit of the new program.

Farm suppliers, laborers, transportation, and other farm-support workers were hurt badly by the PIK program, because the program caused a loss of an estimated 250,000 jobs.[22] Feed prices actually increased because of the bumper harvest, which was a hardship to poultry, cattle, and pork growers who had to feed their animals at higher prices.

In addition, consumer food prices rose. Agricultural economist Clifton B. Luttrell estimated that middle-income families would pay $300 a year more for their food because of the PIK program.[23]

Farmers who participated in the PIK program were supposed to prevent erosion on idled land by planting a ground cover such as sorghum, sudan grass, or nitrogen-fixing alfalfa. However, a survey sponsored by twelve midwestern state agencies discovered that 20 percent of PIK land was not protected in this way, and another 37 percent had "protection" consisting of weeds or crops that sprouted as a result of the previous year's planting.[24]

In the summer of 1983, farmers living east of the Rocky Mountains were hit by the most devastating drought and heat wave in more than fifty years. But, because of the PIK program, some of the farmers in these hard-hit areas managed to survive or actually make a profit. Some farmers sold grain that they had stored on their own farms, collecting higher prices caused by the drought and PIK. The result was that farm income rose to $27 billion, up from $22.1 billion the year before. The drought also cost the government in 5 percent interest drought-relief loans to farmers, totaling approximately $10 billion.[25]

Many farmers continued to have serious financial problems, particularly the younger ones who had mortgages dependent upon the high land values of the mid-1970s. As the land values continued to drop, bankers and lending institutions, such as the Farmers Home Administration, insisted on repayment of loans. As a result, many farmers had to sell off machinery, acreage, or sometimes the entire farm to pay back their loans.

At times angry farmers tried to prevent their neighbor's farms from being sold at auction by the lending institution. They would gather at the farm sale and chant, "No sale! No sale!" until the bank officials gave up. Sometimes neighbors would bid a quarter or a dollar on the item up for auction. Then they would give the tractor or land they had just "bought" back to the farmer at the end of the sale. Sometimes state troopers and sheriff's deputies were called in to prevent violence.

In December 1983, President Reagan signed legislation that would pay dairy farmers not to produce for fifteen months. The government agreed to give $10 for every 100 pounds (or about 12.5 gallons) of milk that farmers reduced in production. Farmers could cut back as much as 30 percent and still get paid for it. The government was already obligated by law to buy the milk, cheese, and butter that farmers couldn't sell. The government's reasoning for the new legislation was that it would be cheaper to pay the farmers *not* to produce than it was to buy up the surplus. They hoped to save $1.7 billion over four years.

Critics pointed to the failed PIK program, arguing that these kinds of support programs ended up costing the government, rather than saving it money. Budget Director David Stockman argued that the new law could force consumers to pay $1.8 billion more for their milk products.[26]

Another new piece of legislation passed in April of 1984, an election year, was designed to woo the farm vote. Producers of wheat, corn, cotton, and rice were paid in cash for cutting their harvests by 10 percent during 1984 and 1985. In addition, the law also *reduced* target prices over the following two years, from 8 percent to 2 percent.[27] (Remember, the target price program paid farmers who reduced production the difference between what the market was paying and the government pre-set target price.) The idea was to lower target prices and at the same time pay farmers to reduce the acreage they planted.

By May 1984, with the PIK program scaled back to cover only wheat, farmers beefed up their production, planting fencepost to fencepost. Farm prices were up, mainly because of PIK and the drought of 1983. Land values were finally stabilizing after several years of decline, and farmers were beginning to spend money again, particularly on fertilizer and seed. Some farmers also were able to reduce their debts to lending institutions, although farm debt was still alarmingly high, and interest rates were creeping back up. But with the U.S. dollar so strong, farm exports were not doing well. And bankruptcies were still very much in the news.

Hard times on the farms were also the motivation behind Farm Aid, a national country music and rock 'n roll benefit for farmers that was televised nationally. Farm stress also was the subject of several acclaimed motion pictures: *Country*, *The River*, and *Places in the Heart*. These movies were very popular and helped to bring the farm problem before the American people. In *Country*, officials from the Farmers Home Administration demanded payment from the financially strapped Ivy family. When the Ivys couldn't come up with the money, they faced eviction. The emotional strain on three generations of Ivys threatened to tear the family apart. The film effectively reminded Americans of the farm crisis, in human terms.

Some farmers with heavy debt loads were not able to get bank loans for seed and fertilizer. Without those loans they had no crops to sell, and their original loan could not be paid off. In many cases, the only alternative was to sell off all or part of their assets, or declare bankruptcy.

Farm debt in the United States was a very serious problem. For the first time in American history, the amount that farmers owed in interest was greater than their total net farm income.

By the end of 1984, federal banking officials esti-

mated that of the approximately 800 banks that were in trouble in the United States, 20 to 25 percent were rural banks that were lending to farmers.[28] Most of the failing banks merged with healthier banks, a move that protected the depositors. But the people who owned shares in the banks were wiped out.

Commercial banks weren't the only lenders in trouble. Many of the federally backed "land banks" and credit associations were having serious problems as well.

Farmers were not the only people defaulting on their loans. Other consumers with businesses tied to the agricultural economy also were unable to pay the interest on loans. Deere & Company, the largest manufacturer of farm implements and tractors in the country, laid off 5,800 workers in Iowa.[29]

The ultimate goal of the federal government was to wean the agricultural economy off government subsidies and turn it over to the free market. Many people, even some in the farm community, agreed with this objective. Farmers have traditionally been fiscal conservatives. But even though they may have agreed philosophically, they feared that any swift course of action resulting in this goal would ruin their rural communities.

In 1985 the Agriculture Department came up with an emergency program providing funds to help farmers who had borrowed from banks that failed. In addition, the administration announced that it would give $650 million to guarantee farmers' operating loans.[30]

Top: Farmers protest Reagan administration farm policies.
Bottom: Almost 80,000 fans gathered to see Farm Aid, a music festival to aid the nation's farmers.

In 1985, between one-third and one-half of American farmers were having severe financial difficulties. This led to widely publicized problems with alcohol and drug abuse. Divorce and suicide rates rose.

The point should be made, however, that the largest farms in the United States were continuing to show impressive profits. *Fortune* magazine reported in November 1985 that 25,000 of the largest farms (1 percent of farming operations which have annual sales over $500,000) showed an average return on assets of 18 percent in 1983. These were the farms whose owners had not bought beyond their means in the 1970s, and they didn't have the tremendously high interest rates to pay as land values fell. And because of their size, these were the farms that benefitted most from government aid.

Also, medium and small farms that didn't accumulate large debts in the mid-1970s, but continued to raise corn and wheat, were making adequate incomes. There were, and still are, many part-time farmers whose chief source of income was off the farm. These farmers, for the most part, were not having financial difficulties.

Late in 1985, Congress passed a sweeping piece of legislation that had the country reeling. The Gramm-Rudman Law stated that the federal budget deficit must be eliminated by the year 1991. In order for government debt to be wiped out, Congress was required to slash government spending, particularly defense and domestic programs. Farm programs make up a large part of domestic spending.

This was certainly a controversial law, and many experts did not expect it to last. Farmers were angry because they were faced with absorbing a large share of the cuts in domestic programs, mainly because programs like Social Security were exempt from the cutbacks required in Gramm-Rudman. Farmers stood to lose $1.3 billion, which was 22 percent of all domestic reductions.[31]

In July 1986, the Supreme Court ruled that a provision at the heart of Gramm-Rudman was unconstitutional. That provision gave presidential powers to the comptroller general, who is part of the legislative branch. The Court ruled that this violated the separation of powers among the three branches of government.

This ruling did not mean, however, that farmers could expect funds to be completely restored for agriculture. The *Des Moines Register* reported on July 8 that Iowa Senator Tom Harkin estimated that farm subsidies would still have to be reduced up to 20 percent in 1987 to meet Congress's deficit goals.

One problem in the farm crisis in 1985 and 1986 was the Farm Credit System, which had been set up by Congress from 1916 to 1933. The FCS is a large and complicated system of bank-like institutions. (They are not really banks because people do not deposit money in them.) They make money by selling notes and bonds to investors, and can offer loans at lower interest rates.

In 1985 investors didn't have the confidence that they had once had, and the FCS saw a sharp decline of more than $1.25 billion in just a few months, between July and November.

Officials of the Farm Credit System announced in November 1985 that the FCS needed $6 billion of federal bailout aid to remain in business. At that time it had $70.7 billion in farm loans, which was about one-third of all farm debt. The loans in trouble totaled $13 billion. This was the first time that the Farm Credit System had been losing money since the Depression.

The spokesperson for the FCS, Ray Moss Tucker, cited $100 billion in plummeting land values as the chief reason for a potential collapse of the system.[32]

The Reagan administration answered that it would not extend aid to the FCS unless Congress would provide for some important reforms within the system. Government officials expressed fears that an unconditional federal bailout would cause commercial banks and other farm crisis victims to cry for a share of government money.

The two conditions for assistance were announced by Agriculture Under Secretary Frank Naylor. He said that the administration wanted Congress to give the Farm Credit Administration, merely a supervisory body, the authority to become the financial regulator and enforcer of the FCS. The second provision was that the FCS would provide for an easier transfer of money from healthy lenders to those in financial trouble.

If those steps are taken, Naylor said, the Treasury might extend a $3 billion line of credit that the Farm Credit System could use if all of its own funds were gone.[33]

At this same time, Congress began debating a new farm bill which Reagan reluctantly signed in December. The Food Security Act of 1985 was the most expensive farm legislation in decades. It provided for a staggering $52 billion in farm supports over the next three years.

The bill froze target prices for wheat and grains used for feed over two years. This was to protect farmers' incomes. Just as in the past, with this "target" program, farmers would be paid the difference between the price at which they could sell their grain and the higher government target price.

The bill also lowered federal loan rates on farm items, which would cut prices for U.S. goods and make them more competitive in world markets.

Critics of the bill raised objections. Many experts feared that the new law would not lead to more exports, but rather would lead to a worldwide commodity price war. Some also were concerned that farmers' income would be reduced by as much as 23 percent.

On the same day that Reagan signed the farm bill, he also signed the Farm Credit System bailout bill. It didn't please farmers, who already accused the system

One Iowa farmer built what he called his
"Reaganomics Machine" to show his frustration
at farm policies. The machine includes rose-
colored glasses and a social-program cutter.

of being more interested in its own preservation than in aiding the people it was created to help.

The new bill provided a small amount of direct aid to financially troubled farmers and an unimpressive bill of rights for borrowers, which included the right of a farmer to review his own file. The law also provided a federal charter for the Farm Credit System Capital Corporation. This organization would buy up loans held by the system's banks that were not being paid off. The FCS was given a line of credit with the Treasury Department, but any additional loans on this credit would require the approval of Secretary James Baker. Farmers didn't like this arrangement because they thought that the federal government was taking away local control of farm funding.

In 1986 farmers heard both optimistic and pessimistic news about their future. There were signs that export markets would be picking up. The foreign exchange value of the U.S. dollar was dropping, which made it easier for other countries to buy American products. And the new farm law cut price-support levels so that the lower prices would entice foreign buyers. The law also directly subsidized exports, a policy that had come under severe criticism by the United States when European countries had practiced it in past years. The law led to early sales of wheat products to Algeria, Egypt, Morocco, and Turkey.

But reports came in during the early summer that a good crop was expected, and that the surplus grain would probably offset any gains made by exports. In fact, so much surplus was expected that experts feared there would not be adequate storage facilities for it. Few new storage facilities were being built. Grain operators couldn't afford to gamble on future harvests. They were afraid that the bins might sit empty in future years and not make money on their investment.

*High debt has forced many farmers
to auction off machinery.*

Meanwhile, the farm land values were continuing to decline, but at a slower rate. The market prices farmers were getting for their crops continued their downward slide. Wheat prices dropped 57 cents a bushel between May and June, which brought it to the lowest price since 1977.[34]

Net farm income had dropped sharply in 1985, and another decline was projected for 1986.

The Farm Credit System, the country's biggest lender to farmers, reported in the summer that their losses for the first quarter of 1986 had *tripled* 1985 losses for the same period.[35] At the same time, record numbers of small banks in the Midwest were going bankrupt.

Headlines declared in July that farm subsidies for 1986 would surpass the $20 billion record set in 1985. Experts predicted that before the end of fiscal 1986, the government would spend up to *$30 billion* to subsidize American farmers! On July 6, an article in the *Des Moines Register* pointed out that the U.S. space program was budgeted to spend $7 billion in 1986. Aid to Dependent Children would cost $9 billion, and foreign aid (including military, economic, and humanitarian aid) $14 billion. "On the other hand," the *Register* reported, "the Department of Defense budget for this fiscal year is $299 billion."

Nearly everyone agrees that there is a need for new strategies in dealing with the farm crisis, strategies that would eventually eliminate government involvement and taxpayers' money. But what should be done? Is it possible to withdraw aid to farmers without causing the ruin of the farm community?

In the next chapters, we'll examine the arguments on both sides concerning government aid. We'll hear from farmers as well as government experts. What solutions are they offering? What policies do they favor? And what do they expect in the future for American agriculture?

What Do Farmers Want?

5

Farmers are a large, diverse group of people spread across the United States. Some are part-time farmers who plant several acres of land and earn most of their income from other work. Others operate family farms that provide their major source of income. And some operate huge corporate farms, earning millions of dollars in profits.

Many experts are beginning to drop the term "farmer" in favor of "producer" or "operator." These newer labels have broader connotations and, some people think, are more appropriate for today's farm manager.

Some operators plant wheat, soybeans, corn, and oats. Some grow cotton or rice. Others grow apples, oranges, and other fruits. Some producers diversify, or grow several different types of crops on their farms; others specialize in only one commodity. Some farmers raise cattle, sheep, or hogs. Others raise catfish, grow sunflowers, or plant Christmas trees.

Bearing in mind all this diversity, one can begin to see why all farmers don't agree on what is best for American farming. Legislation that is good for large, corporate farms may not benefit the small farmer.

As a group, farmers are fiercely independent. Attempts in the past to organize farmers have failed. Threatened strikes in the 1970s never materialized because large numbers decided not to participate.

Farmers can't seem to decide whether or not they want government involvement in farming. On one hand, most farmers say they want to earn their living in the marketplace, rather than rely on aid from the government; on the other hand, they fight for price supports that are supplied by the federal government. In a *U.S. News and World Report* article in 1983, Bruce Gardner, an agricultural expert from the University of Maryland, said, "[Farmers] want insurance against low prices while still being able to take advantage of high prices."

Farmers have traditionally been politically and financially conservative. The farm vote is usually counted on by the Republican party to help elect their candidates. In the mid-1980s, farmers are torn between supporting Ronald Reagan, whose conservative philosophies they support, and fighting his policies that hurt them financially.

Even though there are only about 2.5 million farmers in this country, there are far more people (22 million) involved in agriculture-related industries. Farming is the nation's biggest industry, with assets totalling more than 1 *trillion* dollars. Farming and agri-business are bigger than the automobile, housing, and steel industries *combined*.[1] This huge labor force has tremendous political power.

Most farmers agree that America needs a new farm policy. But coming up with a policy that is acceptable to the majority is very difficult. In the summer of 1983 Agriculture Secretary John Block held a two-day "farm summit." Seventy-five of America's top farm, business, labor, and foreign-trade leaders attended. The result was disappointing. Old philosophies were discussed:

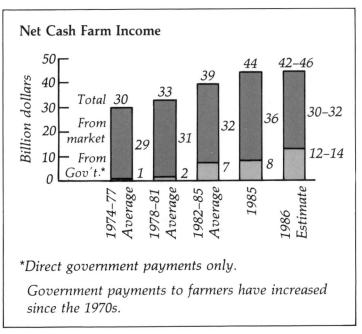

Net Cash Farm Income

Direct government payments only.

Government payments to farmers have increased since the 1970s.

creating new foreign markets, freezing target prices, and limiting subsidies to large operations. The same ground that had been covered many times before was again brought up. No new ideas came out of the meeting.

A *U.S. News and World Report* article in August 1982 stated that "most farmers and their supporters in Congress want to increase food exports, even to Communist nations such as the Soviet Union. They assert that grain embargoes imposed by previous presidents convinced foreign buyers that the U.S. is an unreliable supplier."

Howard Mueller, a "Master Farmer," as designated by *Wallace's Farmer Magazine*, farms 1,200 acres near Waverly, Iowa. He says, "Exports are not the panacea that some people would have you believe; however, expansion is possible." Mueller, who serves on the Iowa Corn Promotion Board, points out that by 1990 there will be 450 million more people in the world. He believes that developing countries will become America's best customers if U.S. experts educate those countries in how best to use American feed grains. He also suggests that the United States provide loans and other agricultural assistance.

Mueller believes that the most effective solution to the farm problem would be a restructuring of farm debt. "If we can't reduce the debt, then we must reduce the *cost* of the debt," he says.

In June 1986, a survey was conducted among 1,340 grain and livestock producers in eleven Midwestern and Western states by the Minneapolis-based League of Rural Voters Education Project. Surveyed farmers were asked what farm policies they favored. More than 64 percent said that they thought farm output should be cut so that prices would increase. Only 24.1 percent favored unlimited farm output, with American farmers competing at world market prices.

In addition, 91.5 percent of the farmers surveyed believe that farmers should be able to vote on what farm programs are implemented. When asked about current policy, 54 percent said that the 1985 farm bill was hurting rather than helping them.[2]

Gilbert C. Fite, in his book *American Farmers: The New Minority*, says that it is very unlikely that farmers will ever form an effective alliance to set food prices at a profitable level for themselves. The reasons he gives are divisions among farmers by geography, outlook, and interests. And, he says, consumer resistance to higher food prices makes it difficult for farmers to achieve prosperity.

Many Americans are not aware that they spend a smaller percentage of their income on food than any other people in the world, an average of $16.10 for every $100 earned.[3] Because Americans are used to spending relatively little for their food, they are unwilling to spend more and are angered whenever food

Many Americans do not realize how dependent they are on the nation's farmers.

prices rise. They pressure government officials to see to it that prices do not rise significantly.

Whenever food prices get higher, consumers are quick to blame the farmers. But what most consumers don't realize is that only about 39 cents of every food dollar goes to the farmer. The rest is spent on such other costs as transporting, processing, and packaging the food.

Farmers have become increasingly aware that they need to better communicate their position to the American people. They are in a business that, unlike all other businesses, cannot set a price for its product that will cover costs and provide a fair profit. Most other businesses with increased costs are able to pass the increase on to the consumer. But the farmer must take the price set by supply and demand.

Weather is another important factor over which the farmer has no control. A long dry spell with little or no rain or a severe hail storm can ruin a farmer's entire crop.

Because the possibility of farmers organizing is very slight and because they can't, as a group, decide how to get what they want, and because many of the factors that influence policy are those that farmers can't control, it seems likely that the same forces that affect present policy will affect future policy. Advances in agricultural technology, the cost-price squeeze, obtainability of foreign markets, federal programs, and the decisions made by the farmers themselves will, in all likelihood, affect farming in the ways they have up to this point. Most farmers hope that, whatever direction farming takes in the near future, the family-owned farm and rural America will again prosper.

As Mississippi Representative Jamie Whitten, chairman of the House Appropriations Committee, said in a *U.S. News and World Report* article in August 1983, "When setting national priorities, we must bear in mind that agriculture is the foundation of our economy. If the foundation goes, everything goes."

Despite their differences, it is clear that farmers have one thing in common: a need for a fair price for their products. That is what farmers want.

Farm Critics: What Do They Say?

6

Most Americans feel sympathy toward farmers. The news media have played an important role in bringing the plight of farmers before the people. Television accounts of farm sales have effectively shown the agony of families who are losing not only their business but their way of life.

Farming has always been an important part of America, and farmers have long enjoyed their reputation of being good, honorable citizens. In 1781 Thomas Jefferson wrote that "those who labour in the earth are the chosen people of God, if ever he had a chosen people." These sentiments have been held by Americans for over 200 years, and continue to influence people's thoughts about the farm crisis.

Many critics, however, think that the romantic image of the American farmer laboring in his field is clouding the picture and preventing people from taking a clear, rational look at U.S. farm policy.

Robert J. Samuelson, in a *Newsweek* editorial in November 1985, writes, "For half a century we have subsidized and pampered farming. By any test, these policies have failed. They have not saved 'family farmers;' since 1940, the number of farms has dropped by roughly two-thirds. They have not stabilized farm incomes. And they have not expanded food exports; indeed, in recent years, they've done the opposite."

Samuelson points out that farm programs help the healthiest of farmers, leaving the smaller farmers and rural banks with the financial problems. Farming, Samuelson argues, should be treated like any other business, since the farms making the most money account for two-thirds of the country's total agricultural output.

Other critics point out that agriculture is the most heavily subsidized American industry, and the amount spent on farming has continued to rise significantly, up to a projected $30 billion in 1986. Also, they say, farmers are the only people in the country who are paid *not* to produce. Is this right? they ask.

Stephen Chapman, in a *Harper's* article in October 1982, reports that official farm statistics can be misleading. For one thing, official figures underestimate farmers' financial health because of the farmers' unwillingness to honestly report their total income. Also, he maintains that farm income statistics include the nearly two million people who farm as a hobby.

The average farm income (in 1982), he reports, was $34,000. And that figure doesn't show the farmer's real worth, since most farmers own an average 400 acres of land, bringing their net worth to about $300,000. This figure, he says, is about twice the average net worth of other American families.

Chapman goes on to say that the decline in the number of farms is "natural and wholly beneficial." He points out that improvements in technology have allowed a smaller number of people to cultivate the same amount of land to feed a larger number of people.

As for the fear that corporate farming will take over what has always been family-run operations, Chapman states that only 8 percent of all U.S. farmland is farmed by corporations, and that the majority of these are family corporations that have been set up to avoid paying taxes. "When you count only non-family corporations, the figure dips to one percent."

Many critics say that the subsidies and tax privileges insulate and protect farmers from the real world of business, and they don't provide incentives for farmers to become self-sufficient. They argue that the recipients of federal benefits begin believing that they are entitled to special treatment, rather than thinking of government aid as a temporary safety net.

Most Americans would like to save the family farm. But critics of farm policies maintain that smaller farms cannot be "saved" by propping them up using expensive federal programs. They say that it is time for the United States to allow the smaller farms to be absorbed by the large operations. And, they say, it's time for Americans to let go of the notion that the family farm must be preserved, whatever the cost.

Everyone Is Affected

7

Farmers are not the only people who are suffering because of the farm crisis. Like the ripples from a stone tossed into a pond, the effects ripple outward and influence their surroundings.

Small towns in the Midwest have been hit especially hard. Farming families go into town to buy household goods and farm supplies. They shop at local stores, have farm machinery repaired at nearby dealerships, and send their children to area schools. A study by University of Nebraska economist Larry Swanson, reported in *The Nation* magazine in November 1984, concludes that if the trend toward larger, fewer farms continues, rural school enrollments will decline by 15 percent. In addition, one out of every ten retail stores will fail, and the number of workers in the towns will be reduced by 7 percent before the end of the 1980s. This will result in the disappearance of many small towns and the loss of as much as $100 billion dollars in uncollected loans and losses to local businesses.[1]

We can, in fact, say that farmers and businesspeople are involved in the crisis together. One economist estimates that for every seven farms that go under, one commercial business fails. Rural main streets just aren't busy the way they used to be.

Farmers spend more money than any other business group. Billions of dollars are poured into the economy of this country as farmers buy needed equipment, fertilizer, and other necessities. Manufacturers of tractors, combines, and other farm machinery have felt the effects of the farm crisis. Deere and Company and Massey-Ferguson, Inc., both large farm equipment manufacturers, have had to lay off many workers. Fertilizer, chemical, and seed dealers have all seen sales plummet in the 1980s.

The ripple effect is far reaching, even into distant cities. One out of every four workers in the United States works directly or indirectly in the agricultural industry. Steel and rubber manufacturers who make products for farm equipment are affected just as the rural workers are.

People in large cities also feel the effect when rural communities die, and the unemployed move to larger population centers in search of work. Displaced rural families not only need jobs, they also require housing and schools for their children.

When farmers and related agricultural workers leave an area, there are fewer people remaining to support local services. The tax rate increases for those people, and at the same time their services are cut back.

Because there is a loss of farming opportunities, young people who had had dreams of being farmers must change career goals. Instead of working the land, they must now turn to agriculture-related vocations, many of which require college educations. As younger people move into the urban areas, small towns begin to depend more and more on dwindling elderly populations.

Memberships in youth organizations such as 4-H and Future Farmers of America are declining. Other

*When economic hard times
hit farmers, other businesses
are affected as well.*

organizations, such as the Jaycees, Masons, and Extension clubs are seeing enrollments drop. Fewer people are attending local churches.

Some experts in rural sociology are alarmed about the future of rural life. More and more land is being bought by people who live elsewhere, and who rent acreage to others or who hire others to work the land. Some experts fear that those who do the farming will not concern themselves with environmental factors and will not care for the land properly.

Similar concerns have been raised about large non-family corporate operations. In fact, many states, most of them Midwestern, have levied special taxes or fees on such operations, or have burdened them with other restraints.

Farmers warn that if large corporate farms take over most of the food production in America, consumers will almost certainly see a jump in food prices at the grocery stores. Farmers also point out that corporations will more likely be concerned with large profits than with using conservation techniques and protecting consumers from the overuse of pesticides and other harmful chemicals.

Rural communities also are concerned about real estate speculators who buy up huge tracts of land for investment purposes. This shrinks the amount of land used in farming and changes the fabric of rural life.

Small agricultural communities will surely see many changes in the near future. We're seeing some of these changes now, brought about by the farmers' economic crisis. Farms will likely continue to grow in size and have fewer owners.

In fact, the one factor small towns can count on is change. People in rural areas will have to adapt to these changes. Farmers will always be needed to produce food for the growing world population. Some may have to become better managers and develop new attitudes about farming if they, as individual businesspeople, are going to survive.

People living in rural communities are seriously affected by the farm crisis not only financially but also emotionally. In the next chapters, we will examine the emotional turmoil surrounding farm and rural families.

First, let's meet Christine King (not her real name), whose family is losing its farm in northeast Iowa. To her, the American farm crisis is an everyday, painful reality.

The Farm Crisis: One Story

8

*It's an oppressively hot day in this tiny Iowa farm commu-
nity. The small cafe in the center of town is air-conditioned,
but the ceiling fans are whirling silently overhead. Three of
the five tables line one wall, taking up nearly half of the
space in this one-room business. Several middle-aged
people wearing work clothes are seated at the tables and
appear tired and hot. Two couples sit at the counter eating
pie and ice cream. They all seem to know each other.*

*I'm here to meet sixteen-year-old Christine King, whose
family is experiencing the American farm crisis firsthand.
They are facing bankruptcy. Christine arrives right on time.
She's blond and pretty, and her hair is pulled back into a
little ponytail. She asks if she's late, explaining she was
busy working on her 4-H projects. The county fair is next
week, and she's taking twenty-one projects. She seems a
little nervous about the fair, or maybe about the interview.*

"Twenty-one projects?" I ask. "Isn't that a lot?"

"I think I take more than anyone else in Clayton
County," she says, smiling. "Everything from farm animals to homemade quilts."

We talk a little about 4-H and the fair, and she orders a milkshake from the waitress, calling her by name. Then I ask Christine about her farm and about what she and her family have been experiencing.

"I've learned something about myself and my family during the past year," Christine says firmly. "I know we're going to survive. We're through the worst of it, and I know we're going to make it."

Christine King lives with her parents and two younger brothers on a 200-acre farm in northeast Iowa. They raise pigs, cows, corn, and a few oats. They also own sixty acres about an hour away which are rented as pasture.

Long before the present farm problem, Christine's father began a personal crisis nearly as devastating. As a boy, he had had major surgery that left him with a disability that causes his hips to gradually wear down. He is frequently in pain, and it is very difficult for him to do field work. Christine's thirteen-year-old brother Jake works on the tractor, and her uncle takes care of the work in the field.

"Mom and Dad would never have guessed when they got married that all of this could've happened. Dad was in good shape, and like all young couples, they were very optimistic. They bought the house, eighty acres, and were very happy. They've always loved farming," Christine explains, with a smile. "Sometime in the early seventies, they bought an additional hundred and twenty acres which were reasonably priced. It was a good decision then to buy the land."

Many details of Christine's story are similar to what we hear in the media about other struggling farmers. When times looked good for agriculture in the mid-1970s, Christine's father invested in some new efficient equipment. "We bought the 'leg' first," Christine says.

"What is that?" I ask.

"The leg is a piece of machinery that raises up about

sixty feet and carries corn up on something that looks like an escalator. There are eight spouts on it at the top that send the corn off in different directions. It's very efficient, and we thought it would help Dad a lot.

"Then we built a shed for the leg, two corn bins, and a stationary feed mill. The feed mill grinds corn for the cows and pigs and runs the feed to the pig nursery and the finishing unit. A pig finishing unit is where the pigs are taken when they reach a hundred pounds. There they are fed grain with higher protein to promote faster growth, so they can be taken to market sooner.

"My parents say that farming looked really good in the mid-seventies," Christine continues. "Prices for everything were high. They received good money for our corn, pigs, everything, and they thought the new equipment would mean Dad wouldn't have to work so hard. It requires electricity to run but no fuel.

"Then Dad built a huge, new shed. It's ninety feet by eighty-seven feet, and it has three parts to it. In the first section, we keep the pigs weighing from sixty to one hundred pounds. The second section is for round bales of hay; it can hold up to four hundred bales. And the third section is the pig finishing section."

"When did you first realize that things weren't going well?" I ask.

Christine thinks a moment, stirring her milkshake.

"I first became aware that something was wrong around the supper table. That's where all the family conversation takes place." Her face darkens at the memory. "Fortunately, my parents never kept anything from us kids. They were always very open about what was going on. My dad started saying things like, 'The bank's riding on me,' or 'It's going to be hard to make the farm payment,' or 'Maybe I shouldn't have built the shed when I did.' I was pretty young then, and I really didn't worry very much. But it gradually got worse.

"I guess it all came to a head in 1984," Christine

says. "We had to sell off our cows and all the milking equipment to ease our debt load. It helped a little, but not very much.

"We hated to sell our cows. Not only did we love those cows—they get to be like family members when you raise them from calves and then train them and milk them every day—but they bring in regular money. Cows are very expensive, but they produce regularly. An average cow may cost $800, but it will produce eighty pounds of milk every day, milk we can sell. The milkman comes every other day to pick up our milk, and every two weeks the milk check arrives. That's money we can depend on.

"It's different with beef or hogs. You have to wait until they're six months old before you see a return on your investment. It's sometimes hard to pay the bills while you're waiting for the calves or hogs to get big enough to sell.

"Selling the cows kept the bank officials away for a little while," Christine says. "We owe both the commercial bank in town and the Federal Land Bank."

"The Federal Land Bank is a part of the Farm Credit System, isn't it?" I ask.

"Yes," she says. "The bank is giving us a harder time than the Federal Land Bank. I guess that's because the FLB *owns* our land. They know they can come in and repossess it any time to get their money back.

"But there's a new banker in town," Christine continues, resting her arms on the table and leaning forward. "Before he came, things weren't so bad. The old banker was nice, and we felt he was really on our side, but he retired. We think the bank was putting pressure on him because of us, and he retired so he wouldn't have to be the one to take our farm away from us. He just couldn't do it, he was really a nice man. We feel badly about that.

"But the clincher came on Thanksgiving Day in

1985," Christine says, shaking her head. "My mother and I were milking cows for a neighbor, and Dad and Jake were trying to get the corn harvested before a predicted heavy snowfall. My four-year-old brother Tommy was left alone for a short while. He set a fire in the kitchen wastebasket. The fire spread. The kitchen was completely gutted. Tommy wasn't hurt, and the fire was extinguished, but not before severely damaging the inside of our house and all of its contents.

"The fire chief told us that in another thirty seconds, the whole house would've caught fire." Christine pauses a moment, then adds, "That would've been the best thing that could've happened. The insurance paid us $23,000 to rebuild the kitchen and clean the furniture. But the Federal Land Bank took all but $6,000 of it.

"That Christmas my family slept on lawn chairs in the basement. The upper floors were unhealthy because of all the smoke. My brothers and I moved in with my aunt and uncle while the kitchen was being rebuilt.

"My parents had locked $10,000 in a safe in our home years ago. It was to be the down payment on a house if we ever lost our farm. But after the FLB took the insurance money, Mom and Dad decided they'd have to use it to rebuild the kitchen.

"And not only did we lose that money, but that snow predicted on Thanksgiving came in a record snowfall. Dad and Jake had only gotten half of the corn harvested when the fire broke out. The snowfall prevented them from getting back into the fields, so we lost half of the crop. If they'd gotten it harvested, we might have been able to make the farm payment.

"Dad prays every night," Christine says. "We just want to be able to keep our house, that's all. But we'll probably lose that, too."

"How has your family dealt with all the stress?" I ask. "We read about families breaking up, suicide."

"I think my brother Jake is suffering the most. He's very sensitive and keeps things inside of himself. When Dad is in pain, he sometimes gets grouchy and comes down on Jake. It really crushes him. And he loves the farm so much. He'd spend all day on the tractor if he could. His grades are up or down, depending on whether there's field work to be done or not.

"I'm trying to get Jake interested in 4-H, just to draw him out a little. He seems to enjoy it after he gets into a project."

"How about the rest of the family?" I ask.

"My family copes well," Christine says. "Once a month, we plan something together as a family. It doesn't have to be expensive. Just some activity we can do, just the five of us.

"We worry about each other, though. There's a crisis hot line number hanging in the basement on the wall."

"Who hung it?" I ask.

"I don't know," Christine says. "Sometime after the fire when we were living in the basement, somebody in the family hung it up. It bothers me that it's there. It shouldn't be there." There is a pause, and then Christine says, "I think my mother put it there. She was worried about Dad."

"Suicide?"

"Yes."

"What will your family do if they lose the house? Where will you live?" I ask.

"My grandpa owns a house he can sell to my parents with little interest payments," says Christine.

"And what will your parents do if they can't farm? Is there a contingency plan?"

"Yes, they're both going back to school this fall on Pell grants, which are grants specifically for further education for broke farmers. Dad is taking accounting, and Mom will probably get a degree in general business,

*The emotional toll the farm crisis
has taken is evident throughout the
country. Here a mother comforts her
son after the family's possessions
were sold to help repay a loan.*

although she could work for the Post Office. She took the civil service exam and got a perfect score."

"And what will you do?"

"I'll definitely go to college," she says. "The Peace Corps interests me. And the Future Farmers of America has a program they call 'Work Experience Abroad,' which is like the Peace Corps. You can spend several months or a year or two in a foreign country, live with a host family, and teach the people about farming. And there are other jobs that are related to agriculture. I'm also very interested in speech pathology," she says. "I'd like to be a speech pathologist at some point."

"How about farming?" I ask. "Does it interest you after all your family has been through?"

"I love the farm," Christine says, her eyes gleaming. "I always want to live on an acreage where I can have animals and at least a couple of cows." She pauses. "We kept one of our cows. She's our house cow."

"House cow?"

"Yes, we hand milk her. She gives us our milk and cream. Mom scoops the cream into a quart jar and we pass it around the family. Everybody takes a turn shaking. That's how we make our butter. Sometimes we buy a calf. They're not very expensive, from seventeen to thirty dollars. We feed it grain and the milk we can't drink. When it's four hundred pounds, we sell it for about one hundred and sixty dollars. It gives us a little extra money."

"Do you feel bitter at all about what has happened to farmers in this country?"

"I feel optimistic for the most part. I don't think farmers have hit the bottom yet. But when I look at the future of farming, I have to think that the situation will improve because of all the new technological advances in farming.

"But farmers around here are angry. They're angry

with themselves, their families, the lending institutions. They're wondering why this is all happening. What will happen if the farmers are gone? Who will feed the world?"

Christine's final question—who will feed the world—is one you hear a lot all over the country today. With an increasing number of farmers facing bankruptcy, can we safely assume that future generations will be attracted to working the farms the way their forefathers were?

As we got up to say good-bye, I noticed that behind the smile Christine had to offer there was at least a hint of sadness. She'd tried to sound as positive as possible about all the topics we'd covered, but obviously many events in her young life had already taken their toll.

"Twenty-one projects," I said, as she started out the door. "Are you all ready?"

The smile was back. "Just about. I wait for the fair every year. It's one of the things I like best about farm life."

Then she was gone into a troubled world filled with a great many unknowns.

The Emotional Toll

9

The American farm crisis has taken a heavy emotional toll on farm families all over the country. There are many support services offered to hard-hit farmers that provide both financial and emotional assistance. However, many rural counselors and psychologists say that it is difficult to get farmers, men in particular, to come in and talk openly about what is going on in their lives. Many farmers won't come for counseling because they are afraid of being seen coming and going from counseling offices.

A social worker in northeastern Iowa who works on employment programs at community action agencies says that there is a need for classes that teach farmers how to find other employment.

"When I talk to farmers about their job skills," she says, "they invariably say, 'I'm just a farmer. That's all I know.' They don't understand that they have developed many skills to varying degrees because they farm. Many of them know a lot about mechanics, livestock, business, ecology. They don't think of these things as skills because they've just become second nature. But they can use their knowledge of these areas in other work.

With help, some farmers are able to transfer farming skills to other jobs.

"I wanted to teach a job search class," the social worker continues, "and include some mock interviews that can really be helpful in learning how to present yourself to a prospective employer. But I was told by a social worker in another agency that farmers would never come to a class, and that if I wanted to reach them, I would have to teach one-on-one, and I'd have to go to their houses. They would never come here."

This social worker did offer the classes, and she found that this was, indeed, the case. Only a few farmers showed up, even though there was a great need in her area for this kind of education.

One problem that farmers face when they find new employment is giving up their independence. Farmers are used to being on their own, answering to no one but themselves. It's difficult for them to get used to having a boss looking over their shoulder.

It is no coincidence that most farm suicides are committed by men. Many farm men think that talking about their problems is "unmanly." They think it is a man's job to provide for his family, and when they aren't able to support their wives and children, they feel they are not men in the eyes of the community. Many of them keep their feelings to themselves, hiding emotions from their loved ones and even from themselves. One of the greatest challenges that rural counselors have is convincing their male clients that counseling is good for them, and that talking out their problems will help them to better deal with their situations.

Counselors say that farm wives are more willing to seek help. Some of these women are forming support groups to talk over their problems and give each other encouragement.

Farm women need the support groups as much as the men. Often it is the women who have the greatest burdens placed upon them. Many farm wives take care of the household chores completely by themselves. In addition, they also help their husbands and children with the field work, help take care of livestock, serve as bookkeepers for their families, and also take care of the complicated farm finances.

Often, when it's necessary to bring in more money, it's the farm wife who takes additional work in town. One woman, interviewed by Joyce Egginton for a *Ladies' Home Journal* article in August 1985, said, "I used to start milking at four A.M., do a day's work in town selling livestock equipment, then come home and do another milking. I just couldn't do justice to both jobs, and I had no energy left to be a mother. I took the sales job to provide money for groceries, but I wasn't around to guide my children when they needed me, and we have lost the communication we had."

As the traditional care-giver, the mother frequently is the one holding the family group together. She feels it is her duty to help her family stay close, particularly if her husband is unwilling to seek outside professional help.

Joan Blundall, a counselor for the Northwest Iowa Mental Health Center, is quoted in the *Ladies' Home Journal* article as saying, "The women I see are carrying a tremendous burden. They worry about their husbands' depression. They worry about their children and how they can help them feel comfortable about using reduced-price lunch tickets. And they realize that they may have to get out of farming, but they have nowhere to go. They are reluctantly having to let go of the dream that the best place to raise a family is on a farm."

One thing women's support groups can provide, besides sympathetic listeners, is information for participants about government programs that can help, whether it be food stamps, assistance with adult education, or financial or legal advice. They can also provide a forum where new farm management techniques are talked over, and ideas for helping with financial problems are discussed.

Family life on the farm is seriously affected by the financial crisis. Many times parents try to "protect" their children from the truth or are simply unable to discuss what they are going through. Their children feel helpless, because they believe that there is nothing they can do to help. Many times they don't even know exactly what the extent of the problem is, because they don't have the opportunity to discuss it with their parents.

It is very difficult for these children because often they are an integral part of the family farm operation. Most farm youngsters, by the time they are eight or ten, are helping to take care of the livestock or working in the fields alongside their parents. They feel that the farm is *theirs*, too. The family has often had an understanding that the children will take over the farming operation when they are grown.

With the emotional turmoil at home, it is to be expected that rural school counselors are finding an increasing number of kids having trouble in school. Rural students' grades are sometimes affected. Some children run away from home, thinking that it will be easier for their parents to provide for one less. Other students resort to alcohol or drug abuse to dull their pain.

The Iowa State University Extension Service has produced a film called "The Rural Crisis Comes to School" for rural teachers. The purpose of the film is to make teachers aware of how their students' stress at home can influence their work and behavior at school. The film has been in such demand for teachers' workshops that many copies had to be made to fill all of the requests.

One teacher interviewed in the film is Mariellen Dietz from the English department at the high school in Nashua, Iowa. She teaches a special two-week unit on

*Saying good-bye to friends and neighbors
is a wrenching experience when farm
families have lost all they had.*

the farm crisis. Students are encouraged to write about their feelings in daily journals. Role playing is also an important part of the unit. Ms. Dietz asks two students to role-play a parent and child. The parent must tell the child that the family is losing their farm. "Sometimes I surprise them and have them switch roles," Ms. Dietz says. "It's interesting to see their attitudes change, and they realize that it isn't easy for a parent to talk about these problems."

Ms. Dietz explains why. "These people have been reared on a philosophy of stoicism. You keep your problems to yourself. When I see this stoic calm in one of my students, I feel a need for him or her to release what has been kept inside. The students think that if they can't take care of themselves, something's wrong. We need, as teachers, to say, 'It's okay to feel these things.'"

Ms. Dietz mentions that the students in her classes who are experiencing problems are filled with insecurities, and, too often, they try to find escape using alcohol. Sometimes others use tears or negative efforts to get attention.

"Some students are seeing their futures disappear before their eyes. They're wondering if a lack of work on their part might have affected their families' problem," Dietz says. "And the classroom teacher often sees and is the first one to feel that something is going on. We need to be tuned in to their grieving."

Ms. Dietz says that when parents are themselves grieving, they have a difficult time focusing on their children. Parents may not notice warning signs that their children are sending. She emphasizes again the importance of classroom teachers being available to students with problems. "School may be the only secure spot in a student's life."

Some school districts are even including workshops for their teachers about teen suicide—how to recognize

Above: Young people in farm families are deeply affected by the current situation. Organizations such as 4-H can help. Opposite: The suicide rate has risen sharply in farm communities. In December 1985, distraught farmer Dale Burr shot and killed several people before killing himself. His financial troubles were about to claim his farm and everything he owned.

warning signs, and what to do if they suspect one of their students is thinking about committing suicide.

Rural sociologists are seeing an increase not only in suicide, but in other violence as well, both in and out of the home, brought on by the stress of serious financial problems.

"We see more family abuse, more alcoholism, even more injuries to animals," says a sociologist from the University of Missouri in a *Newsweek* article in February 1985. "Veterinarians are treating farm dogs that have had their ribs kicked in."

A *U.S. News & World Report* article in November 1985 states that some experts believe that the statistics for rural suicide are much lower than they should be. Many so-called farm accidents are actually suicides, they say. The deaths are staged to look like accidents because insurance companies won't pay benefits to families of suicide victims. "Local coroners and medical examiners don't want to stigmatize the family, so if there's the slightest doubt, they call it an accident," says Iowa State University sociologist Paul Lasley, who was interviewed in the article.

It is clear that the farm crisis is much more than merely an economic problem. Farmers lose not only all or part of their land, but, many times, their home, occupation, and entire way of life. The ordeal is much like losing a loved one. It requires a time of grieving and healing.

But there is help available to the farmers and their families who will ask for it. Local and state agencies have set up programs to aid farm families in many different ways. In the next chapter, we'll look at several of these programs, and see what is being done for families to help them cope with the tremendous changes brought about by the American farm crisis.

Help for
Farm Families

10

University extension offices in every state have long provided agents and specialists who counsel on such wide-ranging topics as stress management, fertilizers, and computers.

In the past several years, state and local social service agencies have offered more help for distraught farmers and their families. Some of this help comes in the form of support groups where farmers meet and discuss problems. Agencies also sponsor job training programs or crisis hot-lines where counselors listen and advise troubled farmers on where they can get help.

In Cedar Rapids, Iowa, at the Family Service Agency, Joanne Dvorak coordinates a program called "Farmers Helping Farmers," a network of support groups around eastern Iowa. Starting out with a core group of 15 farmers in 1985, the program has now grown to include 260 families.

Farmers Helping Farmers grew out of a program offered by a local hospital where farmers were invited to hear a panel of two couples who were having severe financial troubles. Dvorak, a farm wife herself, attended as an interested observer.

"After the panel discussion, the audience was invited to ask questions," Dvorak says. "After hearing these couples on the panel speak, the others felt freer to speak, and the stories just came pouring out: the frustrations, guns being carried around in pickups, farm wives worrying about their depressed husbands. I was overwhelmed. I would never have thought these people would open up so willingly."

A followup evaluation of the conference indicated a strong interest in organizing support groups. "Farmers kept asking, 'How do I start a support group in my community?' " Dvorak says.

Meetings were held to teach interested people how to set up groups of their own. These representative farmers met for several hours every week, and they had learning sessions in group process and listening skills. A manual was put together covering important topics such as stress, financial management, legal terminology, and how to find a lawyer experienced in agricultural law.

"We began having meetings in other towns around eastern Iowa to let rural people know there was help for them," Dvorak says. "I remember setting up a meeting in a small town church where the priest was very friendly, but he wasn't sure we should bother. He said, 'We just don't have a need for this here. The farmers in this area are doing very well. I don't think anyone will come or be willing to talk about problems.' Well, we did have the meeting, and lots of people came. And, as always, after the people on the panel had discussed the problems they were having, one by one people in the audience stood up to share their own stories. After it was all over, the priest expressed his amazement. He said, 'We've been talking about buying new things for the church and other small church business. No one even mentioned that they were having problems like this. This is really a *hidden* problem.' "

Dvorak agrees that the problem seems hidden. "Just drive down rural roads in the area," she says. "The corn is beautiful, everything looks as if there are no problems. But there are big, serious problems. Many farmers won't come to us. We must let them know we are here and go to them. If just one person at these meetings gets up to talk, everyone else will follow."

Dvorak found that farm people strongly support the group meetings. "One family searched for pop [soda] cans along the roadside to turn in for refunds so they could buy enough gas to get to the meetings," she says.

One of the concerns of Dvorak and her staff is that not enough positive information is publicized about rural people. So they have announced a new award, "The Extra Mile Award," which will be given to someone who has participated "above and beyond," giving many hours of volunteer time to helping farmers.

Other groups are aware that farm families need various kinds of support. Donna Barnes, Dvorak's assistant, describes a program her church offered to rural families in the 1970s. Seventeen rural children from central Iowa were brought into Cedar Rapids, a small city with a population of approximately 150,000. The children lived for a week with host families, and they were introduced to experiences that city children take for granted. "For instance," says Barnes, "there are junior and senior high school students in rural Iowa who have never ridden on an escalator. There aren't many of them, but they're out there. We brought these children into the city to learn about things like how to use public transportation. These are bright children," she emphasizes, "they just haven't had the opportunity to learn about what is in a larger city."

This program also arranged for the children to have medical checkups, something their parents were not able to afford. "One child had to be referred to the University Hospital in Iowa City for a heart problem that her parents didn't know she had."

Dvorak says that from October 1, 1985, through Jan-

State and local social services offices and university extension offices have tried to help farm families cope with their desperate situations through counseling and other professional services.

uary 15, 1986, Farmers Helping Farmers members have met with 1,405 adults and 1,145 high school students all over eastern Iowa. She says the demand for such programs has been "phenomenal."

When Dvorak speaks before farm groups, she encourages the audience to look for signs that their neighbors are having problems. For instance, she says, if a family who had attended church or school functions regularly stops attending, they may be experiencing difficulties. Dvorak urges anyone knowing a family in trouble to talk to them and try to get them to talk about what is going on.

Unfortunately, she says, people don't know what to say to their troubled neighbors, so no one says anything.

Dvorak also urges farmers who think they might be having difficulties to join a support group. "Learn from the experiences of others," she says to them. "You don't have to fall into the same hole."

Despite efforts by local agencies, many farmers still don't know they are having severe financial problems, according to Dvorak. "Many people are in the denying stage," she says. "It's like someone not balancing his checkbook, because he's afraid he's overdrawn. Many farmers don't want to learn how to analyze their finances. They've always done business on a handshake before, and they want to continue working this way. But we've found people who, after going through a financial analysis—which, by the way, is a very long and complicated procedure—find out they are in big trouble. Then they at least know where they stand. And, at that point, it's easier to find out what needs to be done to help them.

"I like to think of Farmers Helping Farmers as a return to the old days of the threshers, the quilting bees, the barn raisings," Dvorak says. "This is just another way farm people can get together to help each other."

Another agency, the Job Training Partnership Act, or JTPA, receives federal grant money in northeast Iowa to help train VISTA volunteers in how to counsel farm families. They help these families with such tasks as determining whether or not they are eligible for food stamps and helping farm wives who might be looking for work, helping them determine what their skills are, and helping them write resumes.

Diane Nitschke, the Winneshiek County, Iowa, representative for JTPA, describes other programs that benefit farmers.

"There is a summer youth job training program for sixteen to twenty-one year-olds," says Nitschke. "Young people are hired for temporary positions. They work thirty-two hours and earn about a thousand dollars over the summer. The kids can help their families financially, bringing in a little extra income."

Another JTPA program will send young people over sixteen to school for a year to learn a trade at one of two nearby technical institutes. If the education program requires two years of study, the student is given his second year of schooling free.

"We can assist dropouts in getting their GED's and help them go on to technical schools," says Nitschke. (GED's are exams that students can take to pass out of required high school courses in order to graduate.) "We can also help seniors with tuition and books if their parents can't pay."

Nitschke stresses how difficult it is for many young people to have to abandon dreams of joining their fathers and mothers in the family farm business. Suddenly, they have to think of their future in ways that don't involve farming.

Education is not the only thing farm families can't afford. "There have to be tremendous cutbacks in everything families do," says Nitschke. "They can't go out much, because most activities cost money. There is no extra money for gifts on holidays or birthdays. Vacations are not possible. Kids don't have money to go out with friends during the evening. I know of one family who described hunting under the couch for spare change so the kids could go to a movie.

"One mother I talked to said that summer is easier for the kids, because many outdoor activities don't cost anything. But the winter is a difficult time for young people. Movies, bowling, fast foods, even skating, all cost money that the family just doesn't have."

One important item that many farm families can't afford these days is insurance. Nitschke says that health and auto insurance, which had always been a necessity before, have become a luxury that many farm families can't afford.

It has become difficult for some families to purchase even small items. "Some parents have discussed their feelings of shame at having to borrow their kids' birthday money for things the family needs, like laundry soap.

"The VISTA volunteers work a great deal with farm children," Nitschke says. "Even when children are not included in discussions about their financial situation, they pick up a lot. Maybe they wake up at night and hear their father pacing the floor, or maybe they see him become violent when he had never been violent before.

"And they pick up on the attitudes of their parents," Nitschke continues. "If their parents are feeling embarrassment or shame, the kids tend to respond similarly.

"Kids want to talk with their parents about what is going on, but many times, they don't know what subjects are approachable. They don't know what they are supposed to tell their friends. This puts tremendous stress on these young people," Nitschke says. "Kids get a feeling of loss, of powerlessness.

"I think it's important for parents to bring their children in on their discussions about the family's situation. Kids should be brought to farm meetings. They would see that other people are having the same problems that they are facing. Children need to see that this is nobody's fault. Kids are amazingly resilient. They just need to be educated about what is going on."

It is very difficult for families to change their lifestyles. Many people eat soup or pancakes or oatmeal for dinner several times a week to cut food costs. "It's ironic, isn't it," says Nitschke, "that the farmers who grow the food don't have the money to buy it."

It is often difficult for farmers, who have not had formal training in other fields, to get jobs when farming is no longer possible. Karen Brown, the Howard County, Iowa representative at JTPA, says that many of these people end up in industrial jobs.

"They have difficulty with industrial deadlines and quotas," she says. "Some of my clients who had been farmers are disturbed by what they see as a lack of concern for quality at their jobs. The emphasis seems to be on quantity rather than quality. This bothers them."

Another thing about factory work that is hard for farmers to accept, Brown says, is a lack of input on the overall product. "I have a client right now who did very well initially when he was placed in a local factory. But after a time, his progress report indicated that his level of quality was slipping. He said he felt frustrated at just being a cog in the wheel, and that it was a dead end job."

This kind of frustration, before or after finding other employmnent, can lead to depression or alcohol abuse. "I had a client who was very difficult to place," says Brown. "This is a very small town, and the man's drinking was common knowledge. Many prospective employers didn't want to hire him. But it was the old work ethic that saved him. He was a very hard worker, and we eventually placed him. He's doing very well now."

Brown mentions that farmers who accept help from agencies tend to get frustrated with the tremendous amount of paperwork required and the long wait to see whether they qualify. "In order for farmers to get food stamps, for example, they must list their income and all their expenses for the past twelve months, and they cannot just use their tax information from the past year. This can be very difficult. Record-keeping tends not to be very good when a farmer is in a poor emotional state."

In many rural areas, hot lines are becoming available twenty-four hours a day for farmers or farm families who need information but don't know where to turn.

In Des Moines, Iowa, a program initiated by Governor Terry Branstad fields calls from all over the state. Rural Concern, as the hot line is called, was funded in its first year by both public and private funds. In 1986, money was provided by the Iowa legislature.

Rural Concern was started early in 1985, and received nearly 9,000 calls during that year. By the end of June 1986, it had already received 8,000 calls, nearly doubling its service in one year.

"What we do most of the time is provide a link between callers and support services available in the caller's area," says Fran Phillips, hot line coordinator. "We have a statewide directory and can provide information to help people with financial, legal, or emotional needs, as well as suggest where they can get help with such basic human needs as medical help, fuel, or food."

Rural Concern employs nine operators who work about twenty hours a week. Seven of them are farmers. One is a clergyman, and one is a nurse with experience in mental health. Each person represents a different county surrounding the Des Moines area.

"Two weeks before the hot line opened, the opera-

Extension service agencies help farmers acquire more knowledge in management techniques, lending practices, and marketing and packaging techniques.

tors began an extensive and intensive training program," says Phillips. "People from agencies and resources around the state came to instruct the nine operators in what their programs offered. Then the nine had classes taught by an Iowa State psychologist and others, including the director of psychology at the Red Cross, representatives from United Way, and Human Services personnel."

Rural Concern also employs an attorney who is available about three days a week to answer legal questions. The rest of the time, he gives lectures to lenders or attends other community meetings to answer questions about farm problems.

About twenty times in the first year and a half of Rural Concern's existence, operators have had to deal with callers threatening suicide. The most serious calls have come during the winter months, primarily December through March. "We have a very strict procedure to follow in cases where someone threatens violence to himself or others," says Phillips. "There are always two operators on duty at any one time. If a caller is threatening to commit suicide or do another violent act, the operator who takes the call gets the attention of the other operator on duty and keeps him informed, via written messages, about the caller's state of mind.

"The job of the operator taking the call at that point is, most importantly, to keep the caller on the line talking. Studies have shown that if the caller will talk for twenty to thirty minutes, the situation will more likely be defused.

"The operator has been trained to lead the caller through a series of questions, to get information that might help the individual sort through the caller's problems. He will also try to get the person's address, although this is not always possible. Mainly, though, he tries to determine how lethal the situation is.

"Meanwhile, the second operator on duty will contact the psychologist on the hot line staff. The psychologist is the one who decides what, if any, action is taken."

Since the calls are considered confidential, bringing in any outside help could cause serious legal problems. "Sometimes bringing in help, such as law enforcement personnel, does more harm than good," says Phillips.

Phillips notes several reasons for the increased use of the Rural Concern hot line. First, she says, more farmers are aware that the hot line is available to them. Secondly, farmers are now realizing that they are not the only ones with problems.

"When we started a year and a half ago," says Phillips, "farmers in Iowa were still denying they had problems. You see, farmers have had ups and downs in the market practically forever. They were used to the idea that if the market was bad this year, it'll be better next year. We're past that now. Farmers are now aware that this situation involves the global agricultural industry.

"And farmers know their neighbors are having troubles, too. Several years ago, they were ashamed and fearful that someone would find out they were having severe problems. But there's more acceptance now."

Phillips says that the hot line staff has noticed a shift in the kinds of questions callers are asking now. "We still get the majority of calls from people who are in serious financial trouble. But we're getting more calls from people who are not in danger of losing their farm, but just want to look at their long-term situation. They're asking such questions as, 'Should we stay in agriculture?' Others want to learn about debt restructuring or want to know if they can get out of debt without a deficiency payment. The Iowa legislature has passed six laws affecting farmers this year, and Rural Concern operators are being asked to interpret what those laws mean to local farmers. The callers are trying to figure out the best way to solve their problems."

We have mentioned just a few of the agencies that

are giving assistance to farmers and their families. Some agency personnel express concern, however, that the attitude among those helping farmers is that the "crisis" is temporary.

"We object to the word 'crisis' to refer to this problem," one social worker says. "The word 'crisis' connotes an end to the problem is in the near future. This is not the case. The farm situation is ongoing. A more accurate word would be 'condition.' "

An eastern Iowa woman who has a rural background and serves as an advocate for farmers in trouble says, "I have a fear that everyone is now jumping onto the 'crisis' bandwagon.

"We need to keep the problem in perspective. I know of agencies that have started farm programs that are designed to be in existence for three to five years. The plan is that they will fold up operations when the 'crisis' is over. But this is not a short-term problem. It will not go away in a few years. In fact, it won't cease to be a problem until the people without power get power. And the farmers will have to take the initiative.

"Until now, a farmer has been the 'wee, small voice in the night.' Farmers need to recognize that a single voice will not be heard, but that they have a strong collective voice.

"They also need to recognize their weaknesses and when to ask for outside help. For instance, if they aren't good with keeping figures, they need a bookkeeper to help them.

"You see, pride is a cultural life pattern," the advocate says. "And farmers have a fear of being separated from the land. Many farmers think if they don't admit there are problems, then they don't have to face this fear.

"But many of them deny too long. They aren't aware that timing is important to catch the problem before it's too late.

"Farmers must also become aware that if they hear

It is in everyone's interest to keep
America's farms healthy and thriving.

the word 'foreclose,' it doesn't automatically happen," she continues. "There is a new law which states that a lender cannot foreclose on a farm without mediation. Both the farmer and the lender must attend this meeting. Of course, the loophole is that a resolution does not have to be agreed upon. What is mandated is just that mediation must occur."

This farm advocate advises farmers to keep up on their legal rights. She encourages them to ask experts about the meaning of new laws.

"And, finally, it's important for farmers to be willing to risk *trusting*. At some point, they're going to have to take that risk and ask for some help. Any change involves risk. We cannot live in the past, but we must come to terms with, and be open to, the future."

Clearly, many of the factors that determine a farmer's future cannot be controlled by the farmer himself: the price he gets for his crops, the weather, government programs, and export policies and politics. But the farmer does have control over the way he *responds* to these factors. He may decide to try to handle everything himself, and, if he is "brilliant," as one farm expert put it, he may do very well.

But if he finds that some aspects of the complicated business of farming are difficult for him, a wise farmer will ask assistance from an expert. And many farmers find that this assistance makes all the difference.

Source Notes

Chapter Two

1. Ladd Haystead and Gilbert C. Fite, *The Agricultural Regions of the United States* (Norman: University of Oklahoma Press, 1955); *Yearbook of Agriculture, 1930* (Washington, 1930), p. 942; *1930 Census of Agriculture,* General Report, IV (Washington, 1932); and *1950 Census of Agriculture,* General Report, II (Washington, 1952) as reported in Gilbert C. Fite, *American Farmers The New Minority,* (Bloomington, 1981), p. 29.

2. *Yearbook in Agriculture,* 1930, p. 414 as reported in Fite, *American Farmers,* p. 29.

3. *Yearbook in Agriculture,* 1923, pp. 8-11 as reported in Fite, *American Farmers,* p. 49.

4. *Funk & Wagnalls New Encyclopedia* (New York, 1979), I, 281.

5. Fite, *American Farmers,* p. 65.

6. Ibid., p. 65.

7. Elinor Lander Horwitz, *On the Land,* (New York, 1980), p. 100.

8. Willard W. Cochrane and Mary E. Ryan, *American Farm Policy, 1948-1973* (Minneapolis: University of Minnesota Press, 1976), pp. 326-327 as reported in Fite, *American Farmers,* p. 144.

9. *Funk & Wagnalls New Encyclopedia,* I, p. 282.

10. Fite, *American Farmers,* p. 133.

Chapter Three

1. Gilbert C. Fite, *American Farmers, The New Minority*, (Bloomington, 1981), p. 178.
2. Ibid, p. 179.
3. Ibid, p. 183.
4. Ibid, p. 201.
5. *New York Times*, September 19, 1974, Sec. L., p. 1, col. 6.
6. *Des Moines Register*, January 5, 1975, p. 1, col. 6.
7. Elinor Lander Horwitz, *On the Land* (New York, 1980), p. 113.
8. Fite, *American Farmers*, p. 208.
9. *New York Times*, February 6, 1980, p. 12, col. 1.
10. Fite, *American Farmers*, p. 212.
11. Ibid., p. 213.

Chapter Four

1. Steve Huntley, "Why Farmers Are Singing the Blues," *U.S. News and World Report*, (May 19, 1980), p. 56.
2. Ibid, p. 55.
3. "Rippling Troubles from the Farm Belt," *Business Week*, (July 14, 1980), p. 94.
4. Huntley, *U.S. News and World Report*, p. 56.
5. David Pauly, Frank Maier, Kim Willenson, Susan Dentzer, "Gloom in the Grain Belt," *Newsweek*, (June 2, 1980), p. 67
6. *Business Week*, (July 14, 1980), p. 94.
7. "Protecting Farmers' Sacred Cows," *Business Week*, (March 30, 1981), p. 43.
8. David Pauly, Jerry Buckley, Frank Maier, Pamela Abramson, "Reagan and the Farmers," *Newsweek*, (March 23, 1981), p. 58.
9. Ibid, p. 58.
10. Melinda Beck, Howard Fineman, "The Farm Bloc Tastes Defeat," *Newsweek*, (September 28, 1981), p. 29.
11. "Prosperity in Sight for U.S. Farmers?" *U.S. News and World Report*, (August 17, 1981), p. 45.
12. James Kelly, Gisela Bolte, Christopher Ogden, "Very Down on the Farm," *Time*, (August 16, 1982).

13. Kenneth R. Sheets, "Problems Pile up of Farmers—and Reagan," *U.S. News and World Report*, (August 23, 1982), p. 64.

14. Ibid, p. 65.

15. Ibid, p. 65.

16. "Amid Bumper Crops, Farmers Fight to Hang On," *U.S. News and World Report*, (November 1, 1982), p. 72.

17. Michael Bosc, Linda K. Lanier, Joseph Benham, Joanne Davidson, "A Turnaround Year for America's Farmers?" *U.S. News and World Report*, (May 30, 1983), p. 49.

18. James Bovard, "Fiasco on the Farm," *Reader's Digest*, (April, 1984), p. 150.

19. Kenneth R. Sheets, Michael Bosc, Joseph Benham, Douglas C. Lyons, "Out of the Drought, Winners as Well as Losers," *U.S. News and World Report*, (October 17, 1983), p. 57.

20. Susan Tifft, Gisela Bolte, Lee Griggs, "Farmers Are Taking Their PIK," *Time*, (July 25, 1983), p. 14.

21. Bovard, *Reader's Digest*, p. 151.

22. Ibid, p. 150.

23. Ibid, p. 151.

24. Ibid, p. 151.

25. Sheets, *U.S. News and World Report*, p. 57.

26. "Milk Taxpayers Instead of Cows?" *U.S. News and World Report*, (December 12, 1983), p. 12.

27. "A Farm-Support Plan Tailored to the Election," *Business Week*, (April 2, 1984), p. 30.

28. "Down Around the Farm, Bankers Feel Heat," *U.S. News and World Report*, (November 5, 1984), p. 58.

29. Ibid, p. 58.

30. Susan Dentzer, John McCormick, Rich Thomas, Diane Weathers, Pamela Abramson, Daniel Shapiro, Penelope Wang, "Bitter Harvest," *Newsweek*, (February 18, 1985), p. 52.

31. David Westphal, John Hyde, "Farm Subsidies at Risk Despite High Court Ruling," *The Des Moines Register*, (July 8, 1986), sec. A, p. 8, col. 1.

32. "Hat in Hand," *Time*, (November 11, 1985), p. 71.

33. Joel Dreyfuss, H. John Steinbreder, "Down on the Farm System," *Fortune*, (November 25, 1985).

34. "Prices Drop for Raw Products," *Cedar Rapids Gazette* (Asso-

ciated Press story), July 1, 1986, sec. C, p. 8, col. 3.

35. "Farm Credit Losses Tripling," *Cedar Rapids Gazette* (Associated Press story), sec. B, p. 9, col. 3.

Chapter Five

1. Kenneth R. Sheets, John Collins, Michael Bosc, Joanne Davidson, Linda Lanier, Sarah Peterson, Gordon Witken, "$22 Billion Fails to Spell Relief for Nation's Farmers," *U.S. News and World Report*, (August 15, 1983), p. 57.

2. "Poll: 65 Percent of Farmers Want to Cut Production in Order to Boost Prices," *Cedar Rapids Gazette* (Associated Press), July 2, 1986, Sec. B, p. 8, col. 1.

3. Sheets, *U.S. News and World Report*, p. 57.

Chapter Seven

1. Heather Ball and Leland Beatty, "Blowing Away the Family Farmer," *The Nation*, (November 3, 1984), p. 443.

For Further Reading

Fite, Gilbert C. *American Farmers The New Minority.* Bloomington: Indiana University Press, 1981.

Horowitz, Elinor Lander. *On the Land: The Evolution of American Agriculture.* New York: Atheneum, 1980.

Lieberman, Archie. *Farm Boy.* New York: Harry N. Abrams, Inc., 1974.

McGovern, George. *Agricultural Thought in the Twentieth Century.* Indianapolis: The Bobbs-Merrill Company, Inc., 1967.

Marston, Hope Irvin. *Machines on the Farm.* New York: Dodd, Mead, & Co., 1982.

Sampson, R. Neil. *Farmland or Wasteland: A Time to Choose.* Emmaus, Pennsylvania: Rodale Press, 1981.

Index

About the Author

Carol Gorman grew up in Iowa where she enjoys theater, singing, writing, and biking through the countryside. She is a mother, language arts teacher, and author with four books to her credit. Ms. Gorman lives in Cedar Rapids.